GEARING UP FOR ENGLAND

By James Maloney

Published by James Ian Maloney

© Copyright James Ian Maloney

ISBN: 978-0-9929263-0-4

Printed by Book Printing UK
Remus House, Coltsfoot Drive, Peterborough, PE2 9BF

ENGLAND SQUAD 1990

Back Row, left to right: Michael Thomas, Gary Stevens, Steve Bull, Chris Waddle, Mark Wright, David Platt, Peter Beardsley, Paul Parker

Centre Row, left to right: Norman Medhurst (Physio), Mike Kelly (Asst. Coach), Des Walker, Peter Shilton, Terry Butcher, Chris Woods, John Barnes, Fred Street (Physio), Dr. John Crane (Team Physician)

Inset, left to right
Bryan Robson, Steve Hodge, Alan Smith

Front Row, left to right:
Tony Dorigo, David Rocastle, Gary Lineker, Paul Gascoigne, Bobby Robson (Manager), Don Howe (Coach), Steve McMahon, Stuart Pearce, Trevor Steven

Inset, left to right
Neil Webb, Tony Adams, David Seaman

4

PROLOGUE

Seeing Bobby Robson sat all on his own, on a bench in the hotel grounds, at this early hour in the morning, was a shock. England's 1990 World Cup manager was just about the last person I had expected to see then, and anyway he was normally accompanied by his trusty lieutenant Don Howe, along with various other FA high-ups. Bobby and Don were close friends and usually went everywhere together. It was 6 am, the sun was casting its long shadows as it rose over the gorgeous Adriatic Sea, and I was taking my now familiar pre-breakfast stroll. The only people I would normally see during this routine were a gardener or two, tending to the flowers. I would marvel at the crisp morning air, breathe in the sweet scent of freshly mown grass. I had fallen in love with Italy, and my dawn ritual was just one of countless special memories of this stunningly beautiful country that I would cherish for the rest of my life.

But now it was all drawing to a close. This – Saturday, July 7 – was the last day of England's historic 1990 World Cup campaign . . . and we were in the wrong place. We were in Bari – but it should have been Rome. In just over 12 hours' time, we would be playing the host nation in the tournament's third place match. We should have been in Rome the next day for the final itself, against Argentina. Instead, we had crashed out at the semi-final stage in Turin in that most agonizing of fashions – the dreaded penalty shoot-out, with West Germany coming out on top (and going on to win the final 1-0).

There is nothing so gut-wrenchingly deflating – well, not in my experience, anyway – as losing in this way. Few "experts" had given England any chance of winning the 1990 World Cup; at the outset, no-one was

5

mentioning them in the same breath as the all-time great national side of 1966, which had won the tournament in such dramatic style at Wembley, against West Germany. But now the West Germans had exacted their painful revenge – and the hopes of the English nation, with millions back home watching the team's every kick on television, had been shattered. No-one felt that pain more than I did. I was the team's logistics manager – driving thousands of miles across Italy, transporting match and training kits, personal luggage, medical supplies, golf club sets and food-from-home preferences. Wherever England had played in this tournament, I had driven ahead of them, ensuring that everything was in place for the party of 52 players and FA officials when they arrived at each venue for their next big match.

In short, I was at the very heart of it all. After a fashion, I became a true member of the "squad." I was perfectly placed to witness the unique maelstrom of emotions – the full range of highs and lows – experienced by players and coaches during one of the greatest sporting spectacles on earth. I had made friends with men who would become household names – or who already were. Soccer superstars such as Gary Lineker, Chris Waddle, Peter Shilton, Peter Beardsley, Trevor Brooking, Stuart Pearce, David Platt, the legendary Gazza (Paul Gascoigne) . . . and the late Bobby Robson himself, subsequently to be knighted.

And now here he was – Bobby, the truest of gentlemen, and the man who had led the unfancied England team to within a penalty kick of World Cup Final glory – sitting alone with his reflective thoughts, in the grounds of our Bari hotel. I was determined to savour every minute of this last day in Italy – and what a surprise start this was.

"Hello, Bobby," I said. "You okay?"

"Yes," he replied. "I'm just having five minutes gathering my thoughts."

"Oh, I'll leave you to carry on then."

"No, no, sit down and join me, James," he said firmly. "This gives me the chance to speak to you in private."

I thought: "Oh God. What's wrong? What have I done – or not done?"

But in the blink of an eye my fears were dismissed. I can remember, word for word, what he said to me then: "I want to personally thank you for all that you've done for my team and myself on behalf of the FA."

He held out his hand, shook mine, and said: "You have fitted in really well, James; my back room team and players have spoken very highly of you. Your politeness and enthusiasm have come across loud and clear and it's been my great pleasure to have met and worked with you these past three months."

I had to swallow hard; that was a very emotional moment for me. "Thanks, Bobby," I said. "It's been a great honour and privilege to have been allowed into your camp. I have enjoyed every minute of it and I just don't want it to end!"

Then he asked me: "How are things back home, James?"

"Not good, Bobby, not good; everyone is numb," I replied, recalling the news of a family bereavement that had been relayed to me during the tournament. At this, Bobby put his arm around me. That gesture, and the silence that followed, spoke more loudly than a million words.

The moment passed, and then he revealed: "I'm going to take the PSV Eindhoven job."

In their wisdom, the FA had already told Bobby – before the tournament – that they would not be renewing his contract as England manager. So there had been much media speculation over his future direction, culminating in the strong expectation that he would accept the Dutch club's offer to take over as their coach. And now here he was, breaking the news to Yours Truly, ahead of the rest of the world.

"I've given it a lot of thought and decided it's the best move," he said.

"Well, you must do what's right for you and your family," I replied. "The lads and the fans will miss you."

He smiled, then got up and said: "C'mon, James. It's time for breakfast." We made for the restaurant . . . where Bobby insisted I joined him at his table.

All this – the quiet, relatively subdued gathering of everyone at the start of this beautiful day – was in stark contrast to the scene barely 48 hours earlier, when I had taken it upon myself to organise a party in the team's hotel in Asti. This was some 30 miles from the fabulous Juventus stadium, where England had crashed out in that wretched penalty shoot-out. The return journey from an "away" match always seems to take so much longer when you have lost – and this trip back to the hotel was the mother and father of a crawler.

7

But, with Bobby's blessing, I had been determined to see to it that those spirits stayed at rock bottom not a moment longer than was absolutely necessary. The lads had achieved so much, after all, and it just didn't seem right that it should all end with a whimper. So, way past midnight and after the post-match meal, the party began; the lads could let their hair down a bit with a few beers, which was the very least they had deserved. (The drinks were all courtesy of the FA – cheers, FA!) As the players filed into the hotel lounge, I was heartened to see that they were already perking up a bit. This was not least down to Gazza, who had been doing his stuff in his own time-honoured style, moving around from player to player, cracking little jokes all along the way. This was doubly impressive, bearing in mind that he, more than anyone, had hit an emotional rock-bottom during the West Germany match – receiving a yellow card that meant he would have been suspended for the final, if only England had reached that far. He had been desperately upset – but his mood had changed during the meal.

Once everyone was in the lounge, I did my Master of Ceremonies bit by banging on the bar (with an ash tray, I think) and calling for silence. "I would just like to say a few words . . . " I began, and was immediately encouraged by a round of cheers. I raised my glass and continued: "This is in tribute to a great manager, coaching staff, physios and Dr John Crane (the England team doctor), and a big, big thank-you to the players for getting us so far in the competition, and in the process uniting our country for the past two months or so. From what I have heard from back home, England has been ecstatic at how well you have done." Cue more cheers.

From the bottom of my heart, I thanked the players for allowing me to be very much "part of the team." They were a really great bunch of lads and I had never been made to feel left out in the cold in any way. I was never a great speech-maker, so, to the relief of everyone, no doubt, I kept it brief and concluded with the command: "Let the party begin!"

We sat in groups around tables and the company on mine was Gary Lineker, Peter Beardsley, David Bloomfield (travel manager, son of England player and radio commentator Jimmy Bloomfield) and David Platt. It wasn't long before Gary got the cards out and the drinking games began. As much as I loved my beer, I was never one for those games, so I just let them get on with it. I watched and laughed as they tried to down their drinks in accordance with whatever cards came up. "Spoof," I think the game is called. Peter Beardsley didn't drink – never touched a drop of alcohol – but he had a whale of a time teasing and egging on the others.

I moved around, talking to as many of the squad as I could – a bit as you do at a wedding reception when you're the groom, making sure everyone is okay! One of the longest chats I had was with Neil Webb, the Manchester United midfielder. He and I had already become good mates; we had taken to swimming together in the hotel pools early in the day. He was a very strong swimmer – I thought I was good, but he would leave me standing, or rather, sinking. Now he was not only "down and out" in the wake of the West German defeat, but he was gutted that he hadn't actually played in any of the games.

At least he was to have the consolation of playing in the third-place match against Italy. Some didn't even get that reward. I know, for instance, that Bobby wanted to play Chris Woods in goal for this match – but Peter Shilton was hell-bent on making a bit of history by winning his 125th international cap. Similarly, Bobby wanted to give a game to Steve Bull, the striker with Wolves (then in the Third Division), but Gary Lineker wasn't for budging.

Back at the party, meanwhile, the lads were joined by several members of New Order, the English rock band. They had recorded England's official World Cup song (sung by the players), "World In Motion." After chatting with them, I rejoined Gary and Peter, along with Steve Bull and Gazza. The drinks were well and truly flowing now, and it was noticeable that Gazza was starting to get a little tipsy!

In no time at all, the clock was striking 3 a.m., and at this point the lounge door opened and in stepped Don Howe. "Right, lads," he shouted. "That's enough for tonight." The really amazing thing – bearing in mind the party atmosphere – was that no-one argued. There was no dissent. We all finished our drinks and headed for our rooms, without question. "Total respect," I thought. And Bobby quietly advised me: "C'mon, James, you've got a long drive ahead of you tomorrow." Everyone had been let off the leash for a while – they had well and truly earned it – but now there was another match to prepare for.

For the Bari match, we were staying in Alberobello, a nearby town with a population of some 12,000 or so but still with very much of a village feel about it. More to the point, a scene not far short of pandemonium greeted us on arrival. Many hundreds of its inhabitants had taken to the streets. Mercifully, it quickly became apparent that they were there to greet us – to make us feel so, so welcome – rather than acting in any kind of hostile manner that you might expect at the sight of a rival footballing party.

The crowds also lay siege to the entrance to our hotel, which was guarded not only by police but also by a set of large, imposing security gates. Wherever we had stayed, I had made a point of getting to know the police officers, to minimize the risk of delays in arriving and departing with the truck. So I walked over to them now and made myself known to them. In the process, I noticed three beautiful girls who were trying to persuade the police to let them in. Gentleman that I am, I went over to see what exactly they were about. They were holding autograph books and were hoping to get into the hotel so that the England players could sign for them. This was early evening, so I told them to return at 9 pm – when I knew dinner would be over - and I would then let them in.

Sure enough, they turned up again as suggested. I told the police that it was fine for them to come in – that I would take full responsibility – and I duly brought them in, their faces beaming with excitement as their great wish was granted. The Italians are excitable by nature and these three young lasses were positively ecstatic! We spent some time tracking down the players together – some had gone to their rooms – and the girls ended up with a dozen or more autographs. Then I asked them if they would like to come into the lounge bar with me – and they didn't hesitate; they were having a ball! And it was doing my street cred no harm, either. (They had even asked for my own autograph!) Paul Parker, about to become a Manchester United player, joined us and said to me: "You don't do things by halves, do you!"

I was especially fond of Paul's company. He was always very well groomed and had a grand sense of humour. But he couldn't speak any Italian – whereas I could muster a little. I quite fancied my sense of humour, too, though, and when one of the girls asked me what position Paul played, I replied: "He's the England programme seller!" Their faces were a picture, while I tried not to laugh. At this, I felt a sudden pain in my arm. It was Paul punching me in mock anger. "Programme seller??" he said, to which I replied: "What's wrong with being a programme seller?" The girls were totally confused by now, so I did the decent thing and told them the truth about Paul. A couple of hours later, I returned the girls to the hotel gates and gratefully accepted their kisses and hugs. As I made my way back to the hotel, one of the policemen held up three fingers and said: "You very lucky man!" I just smiled and walked on.

Came the big, final match, and as per usual I took my place at the front of the team coach to wish all the lads good luck as they boarded. Once again, I felt so sorry for them – having come so close to reaching the final. The venue for the match was Bari's brand new Stadio-San-Nicola, which had been purpose-built for the tournament, with a capacity for just over 58,000. (I don't think this match was a sell-out, more like 52,000.) Once inside, the atmosphere was electric. I looked around and saw a sea of flags from numerous nations – Scots, Irish, Japanese among them. I sensed that we were in for a good game of football, and I was not to be disappointed.

It was attacking, end-to-end stuff for much of the match, but it was not until the 71st minute that the deadlock was finally broken, with a goal by Roberto Baggio. Just nine minutes later we equalized when a left wing cross from Tony Dorigo found David Platt. We still had time to win this one, I thought, or maybe it was more likely that it would go to extra time once more. But that theory went out of the window when Italy won a penalty, with Salvator Schillachi converting to give Italy victory.

We had played and lost our last match in this unforgettable tournament – and I felt so sorry for Bobby in particular. How that man deserved to finish his tenure as England manager with a win. Meanwhile, I had a little mission of my own to complete. By a huge irony, Baggio and Schillachi, the scorers of Italy's goals, were two of the players I admired most on the international footballing scene. When we had arrived at the stadium, the Italian coach had pulled in immediately behind us, and I had – rather optimistically – set off towards it in the hope of meeting my heroes. The police and security men quickly put paid to that hope. Now, after the match, I had better luck.

For once, I didn't go straight back to the England coach. Instead, I approached the vicinity of the Italian one and, to my amazement, Baggio and Schillachi were among the first Italian players to be returning. I made straight for them. I stretched out my hand and thanked them, in my Italian, for inviting us to their country and for having made us feel so welcome. They seemed to understand the gist of what I was saying. Yet one more great memory to treasure for the rest of my life. Then it was on to the England coach, and the trip back to the hotel. The tournament was over for us. The job was done, and we were on our way home.

CHAPTER ONE

EVENTFUL EARLY
YEARS IN LEEDS

Much of my life has been spent on the move – either on the road for my work or, especially in my earlier years, moving from one location to another to live. My dad, also called James, was a police officer – hence the early moves. Before his time in the force, he was in the Army. He retired from the military in 1957 – a year before I was born.

Dad was a DCM – holder of the Distinguished Conduct Medal. My mum, Jessie, was also "in uniform" as a former leading Wren. She was a cook in the Royal Navy. Dad won his DCM in the Burma Campaign, when, whilst wounded, he helped defend an administration block against a Japanese force of some 200. Sky TV recently made a documentary about it, entitled "Blood Alley."

I also have a faded newspaper cutting which records this chapter in the Burma campaign, with special mention of my dad towards the end, and it makes me feel incredibly proud of him each time I read it. Here is what it says:--

The story can now be told of the part played by a battalion of West Yorkshire Regiment in the recent abortive attempt by the Japanese to

encircle and annihilate 14th Army troops in the Arakan region of Burma.

This battalion, renowned for success in East Africa and the Western Desert, has added fresh laurels to its name and provided further evidence that the Jap is being mastered at his own game of jungle warfare. During the 21-day struggle east of the Mayu Range, its task was to defend and operate from a firebase established by the Seventh Division.

Men patrolled for information and they patrolled to kill, the latter so successfully that at least 220 Jap dead were counted. The Japs' policy being to remove their dead from the battlefield when possible, this battalion may well claim a handsome proportion of the official figure of 2,400 recently announced when a company of the West Yorks fought their way across a maze of chaungs (stream beds), re-occupied an area secured by Japs and restored the situation.

Many individual acts of bravery during this three-week period of confused fighting are recorded. Sergeant Warren . . . led and dominated the advance of his platoon, rallying his men to keep as close as they could to our own tank fire only a few yards ahead. He went from man to man shouting encouragement to keep them moving on, and when his own rifle was damaged he went back for an automatic and returned to his advancing platoon. He carried on till mortally wounded by enemy fire.

RSM J Maloney, of Edlington, Doncaster, was in command of an echelon area consisting of the majority of the battalion's cooks, clerks, storemen and men, engaged in ammunition duties. Early on February 9, a party of Japs approximately a company strong attacked his area. They ran into the dour fighting qualities of these West Yorkshiremen and were routed in an encounter that lasted only 15 minutes.

This all seemed a world away when, on a gloriously sunny spring morning, I was born in Harehills, Leeds, on May 3, 1958. I was my parents' first child and my early years were spent here, in Barrowby Road. This is the "last" road in Leeds, in the northerly direction, or rather it was, before it was consumed by further major development as the city of Leeds expanded big-time.

It was a very quiet street, just off Selby Road at Austhorpe, at one end, and with a common at the other. My home was Number 18, a three-bedroom semi-detached house, with a large back garden adjacent to fields that stretched for as far as the eye could see. Now those fields are the new stretch of the M1 motorway.

Life was good, growing up in Barrowby Road. I had lots of friends and – on that common – lots of trees and long grass in which to play games and get up to all sorts of mischief! We whiled away the days playing war games, with plenty of climbing up those trees.

I was five-and-a-half years old before I was allowed to go to school, to Colton Primary. So most of my friends already had something of a head start over me. (In those days you didn't start school before five. Nowadays, not only are they at nursery or play school or whatever much earlier, but they're even onto computers well before they're five!) I got on well with my classmates – but not with all of my teachers.

Some of them gave me a hard time – treating me pretty badly - and that was partly to do with my mum being such a feisty character; despite her lack of height, she was never backwards in coming forwards, as they say. She was always only too ready to do whatever it took to stick up for her boy – sometimes, as I'll tell you later, with embarrassing results! And then, after she'd looked after me, the teachers would only take it out on me whenever they got the chance later on, wouldn't they! Actually, more than anything, I suspect this prejudice against my mum (and me) was to do with the fact that she was Scottish, with a strong Scottish accent. They didn't like the Scots in Yorkshire.

And I didn't like the way I would occasionally struggle to get a place on the bus on the way home from school. It was just a standard public service job – not a dedicated school bus – but one of the teachers would come out to the bus stop and cast a close eye over those trying to get on. This bus would travel about one mile to the top of a lane, where I would get out and walk the remaining half a mile, down that lane, back to my home. The fare for this bus trip was one old penny.

The idea was that because other children had further to travel they should be given priority over me in getting onto the bus and having a seat. So the teachers would actually stand there at the door of the vehicle and stop me from getting on. My mum wasn't having that, so she would come down to the school and complain about my ill-treatment. Sometimes the teacher would let me on okay – if it was clear that there were seats available. The kids were fine about it; it was just that one teacher, Mrs Straw.

Coming to school at the start of the day, I would either walk when the weather was okay or have a lift in with Colin White, who lived in the same road as I did and was another teacher (at a different school). He had an old Morris 1000 car which you had to crank up in the mornings to get it going. This was necessary every day, no matter what the weather but especially so with snow and ice.

I remember that he was very fond of his pint – but had to take up golf to be able to get it. His wife Thelma, also a teacher, would not let him go out to the pub with his mates for his ale, so he joined a golf club with the express intention of being able to buy his drinks there!   I went on a number of holidays with Colin, Thelma and their daughters Elaine and Diane, to Scarborough and Bridlington.

Elaine was the same age as me and we became best friends – she was even the first girl I ever slept with.   Mind you, I was all of five years old at the time!   Elaine was a lovely little girl, with pigtails, and very well educated, as you would expect as the daughter of teachers.   We stayed close until we were 13, when my family moved to Cornwall.   I never saw her again.

Another good friend of mine in my early years was John Charlton, son of the legendary footballer Jack and nephew of the even more famous Bobby Charlton, of Manchester United.   Both – Jack and Bobby - were in the England side that won the World Cup in 1966.   Jack was still playing for Leeds United while I was at Colton Primary, and my own early enthusiasm for football was reflected in my selection, on the right wing, for the Colton school team.

This was when I first met John.   I was about ten at the time and John was playing for Halton Primary School against us.   I remember they beat us 4-0 and I played the second half in goal – because our regular custodian had either been injured or was simply written off as no good, I'm not sure which.   John, just like his dad, was playing at centre half.   Even so, he did not have his dad's appearance and he was never going to make it in that position for as long as he lived!   But there's no denying he was tall – and he scored against me, with a header, in that match.   That was the one and only goal I let in.   I didn't actually speak to him that day, although we went on to become good pals.

My other friends in this period included Charles Appleyard, whose father owned the local garage on Selby Road, on the corner with Barrowby Road, Neville Firth, who lived in the next street down from Austhorpe Avenue, Philip Bateman, of Barrowby Lane, and Jimmy McGuinness, my eldest friend, who was like a brother to me.

15

Charles was several years older than me. He was a very practical boy and used to build our bogies and repair our bikes. The "bogey" was a sort of four-wheel plank, which we steered with string. We would play those war games together – us against them, depending which streets we came from – and I also remember feeling very sorry for Neville one summer when, somehow, we had got hold of some darts and were playing chicken with them.

We would mostly have been about eight or nine and Jimmy was getting Neville to dance – literally – by throwing darts at the floor around his feet. Jimmy threw the darts as hard as he could, to make sure they stuck in the floor – except that one of them found poor Neville's leg instead and stuck firmly in his shin bone. Neville definitely "danced" at that. His mum came down, removed the offending dart and took her boy to hospital – but not before giving us the mother and father of a telling-off first. It had been a complete accident – foolhardy rather than malicious – but nonetheless very silly as this was clearly an accident waiting to happen, as they say. I would go spare now if I saw any of my children or grandchildren playing in this way!

On the common, Jimmy and I would build a tree house – only for the others to come along and destroy it. So, in classic tit for tat fashion, we would set about dismantling any of their handiwork – dens and so on. We never fell out over this – it was all part of the fun.

At school, it took time for me to catch up, having started that bit later than the rest, and for some two years I was regularly bottom of the class along with a lad called Graham Bott, who became another really good friend of mine. Just before I had started school, I had an eye operation. I have a "lazy eye" which, if I were to pursue surgery again today, could no doubt be easily corrected now, but these things were not so far advanced in those days and the operation was not a success.

I had my right eye taken out and reinserted after the unsuccessful procedure and so for two or three years thereafter I had a patch over this eye while they allowed time for my vision hopefully to be corrected. My problem was not helped by the fact that I was stuck sitting right at the back of the room – so I was both back and bottom of the class!

There were about 30 of us in the class and one of the teachers would repeatedly ask me, after my failure to come up with a required answer: "Are you stupid, James?" He clearly thought I was daft – which is precisely what I thought of him. I felt like saying: "Why don't you bring me to the front of the class? How clever would YOU be if you were stuck at the back of the class with a patch over one of your eyes?" But of course I never actually said any such thing. You just didn't; the classroom atmosphere was too strict.

One teacher would even go one better and ask me: "Are you blind?" Can you believe that? Convention has it that it is your peers who bully and tease you – impose the mental cruelty. But here were so-called responsible, trained professional teachers treating a little boy of five or six with supreme insensitivity. My classmates themselves were always fine with me; I didn't even acquire any kind of nickname for my appearance. (So far as I know!)

This treatment from the teachers wasn't at all nice; it left me angry and frustrated. I couldn't see the blackboard properly, and I would be very embarrassed when these teachers came out with such remarks, about me being "blind" or "stupid", in front of all the other children. I didn't lose any sleep over it, but their treatment certainly touched a raw nerve; I would rather be thumped than embarrassed.

Even today, I get really angry if anything is done or said to embarrass me. I have always been mentally strong. Psychologists, I guess, would have a field day now with my "case," but in those days you just got on with it. There was a different mindset then (like soldiers coming back from the war and just "getting on" with their lives).

Once I had got rid of that eye patch – around the age of nine or ten – I started to move up the table in terms of test results and class positions. The teachers also became less inclined to single me out for bad treatment. There was one teacher at Colton Primary for whom I had a great deal of respect. He was a really good teacher in my book but, alas, we lost him in very unpleasant circumstances.

He was a really hard taskmaster and everyone feared him, but that didn't make me like him any less, far from it. My liking of him – I must confess – was not unhindered by the fact that he chose me for the Colton Primary football team. Now that WAS important. But even without the football, and due in no small measure to his teaching and guidance, I found myself starting to "grow up." I realised that I was making seriously good progress – with the likes of Maths and so on, with which I had previously struggled.

Then one day, right out of the blue, everything changed and I never saw or heard of this teacher again. I got called into the office of the Headmistress, Mrs Duxbury, and saw that she had with her a policeman and policewoman. They asked me questions about the teacher. I can't remember the exact nature of these questions, but I do all too clearly recall that I had absolutely no idea what was going on. I was mystified and gobsmacked by the whole experience. (Alas, children of that age these days – being more "aware" of such things, rightly or wrongly – would no doubt have had a better chance of latching on instantly to the nature of the problem.)

Anyway, the broad outline of the case gradually became known to me and my contemporaries. It transpired that the teacher had allegedly been interfering with little girls at the school, putting them on his knee and touching them in ways and places that he should not have done. I know he was taken to court, but I never did learn the outcome. For all I know, he could have been acquitted, but either way he never returned to his job at that school. We presumed he had been sacked, but I never heard or read anything about it in the newspapers.

It was all very sad – I had so enjoyed, and benefited from, his tutelage. I was, to use the modern idiom, "gutted" when he left. Nowadays I suppose I would instinctively think "dirty old man," but it was different then. The allegations against him were general knowledge within the school and further afield. I even knew two girls who described how they had been on the receiving end of precisely the misdemeanors that had constituted the allegations against him.

On a much happier note, I remember how, two doors along from me in Barrowby Road, lived my godparents, two spinster sisters called Marjorie and Kathleen Walker. (They actually moved to Cornwall after our own parents moved down there, in 1971, concluding that their lives were a bit too lonely without us!) In Leeds, Marjorie and Kathleen would come round to our house every Christmas Day. We were not allowed to open our presents until they were there with us. Fortunately, they always arrived before the morning was over.

Nevertheless, it always seemed like an interminable wait for them to show. Unlike Cornwall, we often had white Christmases in that part of the world and I remember there was one particularly bad one – it was probably 1962-63 – when my dad had to go along and literally dig them out of their house, they were so badly snowed in. We had some fearful winters in Leeds – and I loved them, of course!

I loved my godparents dearly. Marjorie had been a secretary to a solicitor and I think Kathleen, the younger by about ten years, had worked as a doctor's receptionist. When they moved to Cornwall, they first lived in Penzance and then in Truro, and I'm afraid I have long since lost touch with them.

18

I did try to renew contact with them just two years ago. I found their Truro details in my mother's old address book. I knocked on the door, but no-one answered . . . but the appearance of the property left me in no doubt that this was no longer their home. They were especially clean, neat and tidy people, with great values, and this was NOT their home! Marjorie is almost certainly dead by now, but I guess it is just possible that Kathleen is still alive.

CHAPTER TWO

BITING THE FOOTBALL
BUG – VERY EARLY!

I didn't have to wait long for my introduction to what was to become the great passion of my life – football, and in particular Leeds United. On the rare occasions that my mum and dad used to go out, one of my baby-sitters was Susan Gledhill, a young lady who staunchly supported that famous club. She it was who gave me, at the tender age of five, my first experience of a big, live football match.

The year was 1963 and Susan took me along to see United draw 2-2 with Derby County. I am pretty sure that this was in the FA Cup, probably the Third Round in January, and I do recall that both clubs, unlike today, were then in the old First Division - the top tier, now known as the Premier League, of the English league system. The FA Cup, then, was sheer magic. As a competition, it meant so much more to the fans then than it does now; nowadays it has by common consent been devalued, partly through the proliferation of European soccer. In fact, as many observers would argue, the game is suffering from "too much football" – but that's another story, for another time.

Since that first match of mine at Elland Road, I have travelled all over the world pursuing my love of football, both personally and professionally, and I have visited many a famous stadium and been part of many a gigantic crowd. But no such experience ever made quite the same impression on me as that first visit to Elland Road, home of Leeds United – which I can remember as clearly, as they say, as if it were yesterday.

It was long before kick-off (in those days, long before the TV schedules took over as lord and master of the game, all matches started at the same time, 3 pm, and, apart from occasional midweek fixtures, all were played on a Saturday – none of this Sunday and Monday nonsense tacked on). There were massive queues and we waited for something like an hour to get inside the ground. Even with the kick-off still some time away, Elland Road was already packed to near-capacity, with an attendance of 40,000-plus in the offing.

On a beautifully sunny, crisp day, Susan took my hand and guided me through the turnstiles. Crowds of soccer supporters were swarming all around us as we emerged the other side. There was a gangway to negotiate and then, all of a sudden, opening up before us in all its splendour, was the grand vista of an emerald green football pitch, bordered on all sides by huge, towering stands . . . . and more people, all packed together, than I had ever seen before.

It was an amazing sight – and sound. In fact, I will never forget that sound, even half a century on. The volume was unbelievable. I can still hear it so clearly. I don't recall chants, but there was certainly plenty of singing – above all, an enormous, constant din.   The experience produced the strangest feeling for me. I can't describe it, although it wasn't unpleasant. I wasn't frightened.   I do know some people who have felt positively intimidated, and sometimes even nauseous, when suddenly finding themselves in such a large crowd for the first time.

Susan had brought with her an orange box for me to stand on, up against a barrier, in amongst everyone else standing on the old terraces at the Lowfields Road end, which is now the East Stand. (Terracing was very much a feature of all football grounds in those days, whereas every stadium in the Premier League is now an all-seater. This follows the Hillsborough disaster of 1989, when a human crush at the home of Sheffield Wednesday football club killed 96 people who had turned up to watch the FA Cup semi-final between Liverpool and Nottingham Forest.   This match was abandoned after six minutes of play, with spectators still forcing their way into the ground.   This was the worst stadium-related disaster in British history and one of the worst-ever international football accidents.)

At that Leeds-Derby clash, I had to hang on to that barrier for all I was worth – and the box I was standing on would frequently shake, especially when a goal was scored and the crowd surged forward, going wild with excitement. This sort of thing was very scary for a five-year-old – and yet there was something about it which appealed to me in a big way. I quickly concluded that I wanted more of this!

I've long since forgotten the result of the replay, assuming that that match was in the FA Cup. Leeds, very much on the rise during my childhood years, were emerging as a force to be reckoned with in English soccer and were rarely knocked out of the Cup in the early stages. In those days, hardly a season went by without a genuine giant-killing act – with a top team being knocked out by a "minnow" side from a much lower league. Now, even if European competition isn't the preoccupation, clubs will think nothing of deliberately fielding a greatly weakened side in the competition, protecting their best players for action in the League, which has the greater financial implications and rewards.

In my early formative years, Susan Gledhill took me to see many more Leeds United matches. It quickly became a bug for me and I just couldn't wait for the next match. If Susan couldn't take me, then Dad would stand in for her. He wasn't as keen as I was, preferring to take an interest from a distance - but his best friend, Pip Spencer, was a keen fan.

The pair had served in the Army and Police together. Quite often they would be together at Elland Road when I needed Dad to take me there. There was an unhappy ending to one such outing, circa 1966. After the match, the three of us walked along Elland Road to the point where Pip had left his car, a pride-and-joy old Wolseley – but now there was no sign of it. A car in the care of two policemen had been stolen! Well, it prompts a smile now, but I'm sure Pip was none too happy at the time – and I'm sure every policeman in Leeds would have been on the lookout for it! (Sorry, can't recall the outcome.)

My early football interests stretched north of the border, thanks partly to my mum coming from Berwick-upon-Tweed. We used to go up there twice a year to visit relatives, including my grandmother, Violet Williamson, who was a lovely old lady. She was very strict (a bit like my mum), but everyone had a lot of respect for her.

Mum, in fact, had a brother called Bobby Bell, who used to play for Berwick Rangers, Northampton and Ipswich Town. My cousin Robert - a year older than me and the son of my mum's sister Norma – was a Glasgow Rangers supporter. One year, when I would have been 12 or 13, there was a fete and big open day at Berwick Rangers (Sheilfield Park) and Robert and I went along to it. In goal for Berwick at that time was the great Jock

Wallace, who went on to manage "the" Rangers (I'm talking Glasgow, for the uninitiated!).

Jock became one of Scottish football's best-known and most successful coaches. Earlier, he had clocked up the unique distinction of being the only player ever to play in the English, Welsh and Scottish Cups in the same season (playing for Hereford United in the English and Welsh competitions before transferring to Berwick). Jock was in goal for Berwick when they beat Glasgow Rangers in one of the biggest-ever giant-killing acts in Scottish FA Cup history.

At the Berwick open day, Jock had the slightly less taxing challenge of keeping goal against up-and-coming young penalty takers, i.e. myself and Robert, along with a great many others. For a shilling, we got the chance to take a spot-kick against the great man. Would you believe, we both scored past him! I hit it hard and low to his right, as close as possible to the post as I could, just as another legend, Jack Charlton, had advised (see later). To say I was "chuffed" would be the understatement of the year. I was convinced I had beaten him fairly and squarely. Honesty does compel me to add, however, that with the passing of time I did begin to wonder whether Jock just might have deliberately let me score – as Robert and others had also managed to do!

Whatever, Jock said "well done," shook my hand and patted me on the back. It had all happened out there on the hallowed turf of the Berwick pitch, in the actual goalmouth. In my eyes, I struck a good penalty – cleanly and sweetly. Would a boy of just 12 or 13 really have possessed the power and pace in his shooting to beat such a great goalkeeper? Either way, that shilling was certainly a price worth paying for my claim to fame!

Robert was one of quite a large clan of ours north of the border. There was my Auntie Joyce (Bobby Bell's wife), Auntie Norma and Uncle Tommy, Auntie Mary and Uncle Michael and my cousins Kevin and David White. Kevin had trials with Liverpool but decided to join the Royal Marines instead! Robert had a couple of sisters, Heather and Jacqueline. Auntie Norma and Uncle Tommy had a son, Robert Laidlaw, while Auntie Elizabeth and Uncle Alex had three children – Kirsty, Alec and Lindsey.

My mum had another brother, Albert, who died in a Japanese prisoner-of-war camp in the Second World War. He was starved to death, and my mum and grandmother held that against the Japanese for the rest of their lives; they just could not forgive them. My dad repeatedly wrote to the Japanese Embassy seeking an apology, but all to no avail.

CHAPTER THREE

NEW SCHOOLS . . . AND JACK CHARLTON COACHES ME!

Shortly after my tenth birthday, I moved to a new school – and I do mean new! It was as different as chalk and cheese when compared with Colton Primary. Austhorpe Primary School was a brand new, state-of-the-art affair, that had been built much closer to where I lived. I didn't really want to leave Colton. I had made so many friends there, but of course I soon made new ones at Austhorpe.

Colton was a very cramped school, with railings all around it, giving it the appearance of a prison, and must have been well over a hundred years old. It has since been demolished, I learnt recently. When I was there, it still had the old wooden desks with ink wells, and I duly carved my name onto my desk, with a clay modelling tool, just as countless others had done before me. That school was so old-fashioned and in the winter it was a very cold place – it had heating, but it seemed to take forever to come on stream. The toilets were outside, too, so you didn't hang around there in the winter (although they did build a new indoor block shortly before I left).

I was a milk monitor at Colton – which again was a popular role in the summer but not so much in the winter. Everyone volunteered for this job because it got you out of class! Provided your behaviour had been good, you had an excellent chance of being selected for a week's milk monitoring.

There were about 30 children in each class, and two of them would have the task of going out to a part of the play yard where the milkman had left his supplies for the school. Then each monitor would pick up a crate containing 12 half-pint bottles and deliver them to their classroom. As I say, in the summer, you took your time; in the winter, you did it with lightning-fast efficiency!

That was in the days when free school milk at the primaries was still a fact of life. In 1971, Margaret Thatcher, then Education Secretary and future Prime Minister, was famously dubbed "the milk snatcher" when her Conservative government scrapped free school milk for the over-sevens.

I was a milk monitor at both the primary schools I attended. In contrast to Colton, Austhorpe was large, spacious, warm and comfortable – and absolutely everything was brand new, of course. It had modern desks and teaching facilities and better play areas. The grass for the football pitch hadn't even grown yet! On the down side, though, I lost my good mate Graham Bott. He stayed at Colton. Many years later, when I paid a return visit to Leeds, I tried without success to renew contact with him. It was a shame, because he was a really good pal.

The new Austhorpe school was just half a mile away from my home in Barrowby Road. This was the academic year 1969-70, and that Christmas I fell victim to what I consider to have been very harsh "disciplinary action" affecting my football. I loved my sport – especially my football – and I was also involved in the school Christmas concert. We were singing carols and two of us had mischievously changed the wording slightly for one of them; I think it was "Silent Night." The changes were nothing obscene and I doubt if more than a handful of people would have noticed, let alone bothered. But someone was sufficiently observant and concerned enough to report us. We got sent to the Headmaster – who, knowing how much I loved my football, promptly banned me from playing football over the next two terms (plus, for good measure, from taking part in the School Sports Day). As I say, a trifle harsh, I think you might agree.

This punishment was doubly unfortunate, in fact, as my mum had just bought me a brand new soccer kit – shirt, shorts, stockings and boots, which never did come cheap, even in those days. I had played just one game for this school at that stage (losing 3-2 to Holton again, with John Charlton once more against me), and the punishment hit me really hard. I never had the heart to tell my mum about it, given that she had just bought all that expensive new kit for me.

So what did I do? So far as she was concerned, I was still playing for the school team. I only went to extreme lengths to get mud all over that kit each time I was supposed to have been playing, didn't I! Yes, that's me, the son of a policeman father and a very strict mother, pulling the wool over their eyes in such "criminal" fashion. That common had so many uses. On my way home on match days, I would find no shortage of mud in there. Luckily, the school team was not actually competing in a league, so there were only so many games to consider. All my pals knew what was going on and had a good laugh, but we were a loyal bunch and no-one grassed on me.

So that was it – just the one match for my new Austhorpe school team. During that academic year, I passed my 11+ Exam, but big changes were underway in the education system and the old business of grammar or secondary modern schools was being done away with. My next school was a brand new comprehensive, under the name of John Smeaton, after the accomplished civil engineer. Smeaton (1724-92) was actually born in Austhorpe and his most notable achievements included the rebuilding of the Eddystone Lighthouse, off Plymouth, and construction of the great Forth and Clyde Canal in Scotland.

Once again, then, I found myself in a brand new, state-of-the-art school. At that particular moment, there was probably no other school in Britain that was so modern, in all senses. We were the first year there in more ways than one. There was actually no-one else there at the start – just us, with other year groups subsequently following us every 12 months (and with pupils in the years ahead of us seeing out their time at the grammars and secondaries).

Talk about "space age," or that's how it seemed to me at the time. The sports facilities – my big interest, remember – included all-weather football pitches and even FLOODLIGHTS! Magic. You just didn't have such things at schools in those days. There was also a heated indoor swimming pool – more luxury! – and, for the first time in my short life, trays with individual compartments for starter, main course and puddings for our meals in the spanking new canteen. The only problem was that we had to eat fast or else the later parts of our meal would start to go cold!

I was put into the "White 3" first year class, with a lovely teacher by the name of Miss Robinson, who would have been in her mid- to late 20s. In fact, I found all the teachers there to be a fantastic bunch. My days of problems with teachers were now well and truly behind me. At John Smeaton, I also learnt to play rugby league and take part in cross-country running. I represented the school at both cross-country and my first love, soccer.

Did I say "magic" just now? It got even better when I realised that one of my all-time heroes, big Jack Charlton, would be coaching the school football team (courtesy of his link to the school via his son John, who was also there now). Every Monday, after school, Big Jack would be there, out on the pitch imparting his wisdom to us. You'd have to be a football fan to understand EXACTLY how I felt at this point. I'd been following my beloved Leeds United since I was five, and now here was one of those living legends, coaching ME, in these fabulous new facilities at my new school.

He would also be there, watching from the touchline, when our school team played their matches, during lesson time. His coaching was fantastic. He was very strict with us – he really put you through your paces. Fitness was his big thing. I can see him standing there now, with a cigarette in his mouth (I kid you not), watching us and urging us on as we ran round and round that pitch, probably ten times each session. He would also have us doing press-ups, sprints and "weaving ball" – dribbling in and out of cones. None of us had ever trained like this before – and as bonus for me, my friendship with John Charlton was simultaneously blossoming.

I particularly remember Jack's advice concerning corners. He wanted the ball to be delivered as close as possible to the six-yard line. This would cause maximum problems for the defending team and would enable the likes of me to rush in from the edge of the penalty area to meet that incoming ball.

You will have gathered that I was and am a big, big fan of Big Jack, holding him in the greatest awe. Not so my mum, however, as per one never-to-be-forgotten incident arising from an extended training session early one Monday evening. It was the middle of winter, so darkness took over early. Someone had done something to upset Jack and so, in time-honoured football fashion, he ordered extra training. In our case, this meant an extra half an hour.

I loved my training session with Jack so much that this hardly hurt . . . except that it resulted in my having to walk home, arriving at around 6.30 pm. My poor mum had worked herself up into a terrible state, being beside herself with worry. She gave me absolute hell. She thought I had been dawdling, or gone off playing somewhere, on the way home. When she eventually calmed down, I explained what had happened, adding that as a result I had had to walk all the way home after missing my bus. I kept insisting "Jack kept us behind; Jack kept us behind," and in the end she did believe me. But if I thought that was the end of the matter, I had another think coming.

The following Monday, just as we were all lining up for the start of our weekly session with Jack, I suddenly spotted my mum striding onto the training pitch and making a bee-line for him. It ended up quite a sight, with my mum, barely five feet tall, waving her finger and shouting up to this giant of a man. The name Jack Charlton meant nothing to her – it didn't matter if he was the King of England, she was not remotely intimidated by him. All that mattered to her was that he was the guy who had made her boy come home late, in the dark. She duly tore into him: "Don't you ever keep my boy in late like that again. You made him miss his bus and he had to walk home three miles in the dark."

"Fiery little Scot" is the term that springs to mind for Mum, and that description was never more apt as Big Jack stood there, seemingly paralysed and powerless. I was so embarrassed. I could feel the eyes of all my fellow footballers on us – Jack, Mum and me. I was acutely aware that there were 20-odd boys there who must all have been thinking: "James' mum is holding up our training session." They must also have been wondering what exactly my mum was saying, on account of her heavy Scottish accent. Jack would have understood it okay as a Geordie. He was seemingly spellbound, remaining speechless while my mum was saying her piece. At one point, he did look across to me and our eyes met – but he stayed silent and expressionless. This was all the more remarkable for the fact that Jack was known for his anger – you didn't mess around with him.

In fairness to my mum, I can understand her concern because there had been a couple of nasty murders in Leeds roundabout that time, on top of which the "Moors murders" were still fresh in the mind. (These – the deaths of five children aged ten to 17 – were carried out by Ian Brady and Myra Hindley between 1963 and 1965 in and around what is now Greater Manchester. Hindley was characterised by the press as "the most evil woman in Britain.") Mum would worry – really worry. In those days, there were no mobile phones. Heck, we didn't even have a land line in our house! We had to use a kiosk up the road.

Throughout her tirade, Mum didn't swear at Jack; she just ranted and raved at him. Once she stopped to catch her breath, Jack gave her a sincere and heartfelt apology. He "hadn't realised" – and he promised it would never happen again. They ended up both laughing and smiling – some sort of banter, I guess, between Scots and Geordies - but I feared: "That's it; that's the end of my football days here." To his credit, Jack never took it out on me in any way. I was still in the team for the following week's match . . . and I never missed that bus again!

Jack never once even mentioned the incident at all to me, let alone held a grudge against me. Even better, a few weeks later he brought in a brand new Leeds United tracksuit for me (maybe as a sop to my mum?). The decades have gone by since then, and yet I still occasionally come across an old team-mate who will say: "Do you remember that time when your mum took on Jack Charlton?" "How could I ever forget it?" I reply.

I was only at John Smeaton for two years, as my family were on the move again in June, 1971. Even so, as well as my football and cross-country exploits, I also won a "merit card" award for my design for a house. I took quite a strong interest in architecture at that time, but this was not something I subsequently pursued. For one thing, Maths was never my strong point; for another, life is too short for everything that you want to do!

They gave me a good send-off from that school. On my last day there, we were all sitting in the common room, with its comfortable couches and lovely soft furnishings, when everyone else suddenly left. One of the teachers told me to stay precisely where I was, not to move. A few minutes later, they all returned – complete with a collection of presents for Yours Truly, to mark my leaving. I was overwhelmed. I was given books and lots of sweets and chocolates, but what I treasured most, funnily enough, was a stapler – I had not had my own stapler before, and only teachers had them in those days. So this was definitely a rise up the status ladder!

CHAPTER FOUR

MY NEW LIFE IN CORNWALL

Mum and Dad kept the news from their children for as long as they could, regarding the upcoming move to Cornwall. In my case, I think they were all too aware of just how reluctant I would be to leave Leeds – and in particular my beloved United football team. It was just two short weeks from announcement to departure.

There was so much that I would miss. I was such a passionate Leeds soccer fan that I would think nothing, all on my own at the age of 11, of walking the two miles or so from the city centre to that magical Elland Road ground, and then back again after the match. (I would catch a bus for the five miles each way between home and city centre.) Along the way, I would walk through bombed out housing estates, with the aftermath of the Second World War by no means fully consigned to history. Even then, a quarter-century later, Britain's cities were still in the process of being rebuilt.

I would usually buy myself some sweets in the markets en route to Elland Road. I got quite street-wise, in fact, learning which ones were okay and which ones to avoid. I always wore my Leeds colours, with pride. One of the matches I was looking forward to more than most was between Leeds and one of the biggest names in European football, the mighty Juventus. This was in the old Inter Cities Fairs Cup (now the Europa Cup), and the second leg of the final. The teams had drawn 0-0 in the first leg in Italy. I queued for something like four hours for my ticket for this match.

My parents, too, knew I had done this, and just how much this match meant to me. (From memory, my queuing had even been done on a weekday, meaning that I had played truant . . . and I'm pretty sure my parents knew this, too, but chose to turn a blind eye.) Hence one more reason for them not telling me about the move away – to Cornwall – until the last possible moment because, unfortunately, the move meant that I would MISS this match! The match took place on June 3, 1971, and we were upping and offing that very day.

Leeds won that second leg 1-0 to take the cup . . . but the nearest I got to it, cruelly, was when our train passed the club's training ground that morning – and I could see the Leeds players preparing for the big night. A week earlier, my mum and dad had jointly announced that we would be moving to Cornwall, in line with Dad's promotion to police sergeant, to live at a little hamlet called Bridge, which is near Portreath on the north coast. Would you believe, I had never even heard of Cornwall at that stage!

I was absolutely gutted; I could not believe it. So far as I was concerned, I was having a wonderful life. It would be like leaving a "family" – my beloved city and its great football team, along with all the mates I had grown up with. I told Mum and Dad that I didn't want to go, but of course I had no choice.

We arrived in Bridge after a journey of some 12 hours, most of it on the train. I was still clutching my Juventus ticket (which I still have, to this day, 40-plus years on). That cup final second leg was about to kick off within minutes of our arrival at our new home, which was, for the time being, one of two little chalets built into the grounds of a large manor-type property called Fairfield House. This was to be our temporary home while a new house, also in Bridge, was being built. (Alas, that move was delayed, as a result of the builders going bust.) Being in this chalet felt a bit like being on holiday – but I was totally preoccupied with thoughts of that football match. All I wanted to do was find a radio to listen to the commentary.

But there would have been no joy in that direction anyway, because I remember a huge man – our landlord, an ex-seaman – telling me: "You can't get any reception here, lad." "WHAT?" "There's no reception here." Cue panic stations. I had only been here a few minutes and already I hated the place! The year was 1971, remember, so there were no such things as mobile phones or the internet. We still didn't even have a land-line phone. There was no live football on the telly in those days except for the World Cup. *Match of the Day* gave us recorded highlights on Saturday night – and that was it! This was a Wednesday evening in a "foreign" land . . . with no radio reception.

I got hold of *The Sun* newspaper the next day, but it didn't even have the result, let alone a match report. Not even any coverage of the early stages of the match. I asked around, but no-one knew the result – few even seemed to be remotely interested. It was, after all, very much rugby territory down here in Cornwall. It was Friday before I finally got the great news – in a newspaper – that I had so desperately sought.

Meanwhile, as time wore on, it gradually became apparent that the world had not, after all, come to an end. On our first morning there, in fact, I discovered that we had moved to a place that was, by comparison with Leeds, an incredibly beautiful location. Until then, apart from our visits north of the border, I had only known big-city life. I could not believe just how beautiful this new place was. I went exploring with my sister Caroline (who was three years younger than me, having been born in 1961). By the end of that first day, I had fallen in love with it all! We had been to Scotland enough times, but this was a very different kind of beauty – and it all helped take my mind off that football match. A little.

That first day also included my first experience inside a pub. Mum and Dad took us into the Bridge Inn (which is still there today). We had never been allowed inside a pub before; Dad would tell us to stay outside, and he would bring packets of crisps out to us. Now we were on the inside – and we all had Cornish pasties, which was another first for me. I loved it – and I've had one or two more of them since. Like, probably a thousand or so, all over the place! Until then, the nearest thing I had ever had to a pasty was a sausage roll. I've had some great pasties – and some poor ones. One of the best places used to be Berryman's in Redruth.

I quickly got "in" with some new mates at Portreath, playing football with them and so on and making this new boy feel really welcome, and they helped me in my choice of new school, which boiled down to either Tolgus Secondary Modern or Redruth Grammar. Their friendship was doubly welcome, considering that I was the only "foreigner" among them with a strange accent, but then again it's a fact that sport the world over brings people together. All these Cornish lads went to the Tolgus school, so that's where I plumped for, even though I had passed my 11+. My parents didn't stand in my way, although I suspect that their awareness of just how upset I had initially been at moving to Cornwall may have had something to do with that!

I never regretted my choice for one minute. I remember my mum and dad taking me along to see the headmaster, Mr Wiseman, a very nice chap who told me: "You will probably find the children here a bit slow," and I thought: "Oh good, we'll be on the same level, then!" I didn't try to understand why he had said that; I just felt chuffed that I would be "fast." There was hope for me yet!

Back home, we were on the move again before very long, after the builders of our new house had gone bust. This obviously meant a delay in moving into that one, but in the meantime our chalet was pre-booked by incoming holidaymakers at the height of the season, and so we had to transfer elsewhere. At one stage, we even found ourselves living in a two-berth caravan in the garden of the Portreath Post Office! Caroline and I thought this was all very exciting. It was anything but satisfactory in the greater scheme of things, but we didn't mind – we were on an adventure and it all helped take our mind off the disappointment of leaving Leeds.

It was a gorgeous summer, that year, and we had discovered the joys of the lovely golden beach at Portreath – we were swimming there virtually every day. Could kids be happier? I had already learnt to swim, incidentally, when I had fallen, fully clothed, into an outdoor swimming pool in Scarborough. There was no need for my dad, who was with me, to jump in and rescue me. I took to it literally like the proverbial duck to water, instantly learning to swim and haul myself out again, with no hint of panic. I even went on to swim for the Leeds city team at the age of 11, in the freestyle event.

As for my schoolmates at Tolgus, they were NOT slow – but a lot of them did become lifelong friends, and little did I realise at the time that I was rubbing shoulders with some real stars of the future in the rugby world. Among them was Harold Stephens, who went on to play for England at rugby, Roger Harris, hooker for Penryn and Cornwall, Terry Pryor, who played for Redruth, Cornwall and even the Barbarians, plus one of my most long-lasting mates of them all, Graham Still, who played for Redruth, Ebbw Vale, the RAF, Police and England B. Yours Truly represented Tolgus at football, rugby and cross-country running.

My best friend at Tolgus was David Laity, who was a staunch supporter of the Liverpool football team. That made it "interesting," you might say, given that Liverpool and my Leeds United were deadly rivals at the higher end of the English soccer tree back then, in the early 1970s. David was the same age as me, but somehow always seemed older. He had a big physique and a really mature intellect, and we just hit it off beautifully. We remain in regular contact, and at the time of going to press he is working as a sales representative for the John Hindes gift company, based on Redruth's Cardrew Industrial Estate.

Having come from the world of rugby league in Leeds, I had to adapt to the other "code", rugby union, in Cornwall. As much as anything, that meant getting used to not holding on to the ball. In rugby league, the doctrine was: "don't get rid of the ball." It took me a long time to grasp the different rules, which caused much frustration for my teachers and mates. Being small (just 5ft 2ins tall and not carrying much weight) and fast, I played on the wing in both rugby and football.

In early 1972 I was on the move again, this time to more "permanent" accommodation in Camborne, where new police houses had been built in a development called Treswithian Parc. For me, it was another gut-wrenching experience. Once again, I was having to say goodbye to a whole bunch of newly-acquired mates; I had to leave Tolgus and start anew at Camborne Comprehensive School.

Once again, though, I settled in quickly and everything was pretty good . . . until the time came for me to play rugby for my new school against the Tolgus team, i.e. against my previous mates. I got the **** kicked out of me. Things never actually got nasty, but they made very sure that their former colleague came in for a right good pummelling! And they won the match, too, as they so often did, given the calibre of player they had, as I outlined a few paragraphs ago.

I was at the Camborne school for about six months, following which, would you believe, we were on the move yet again. This time it was back to Portreath, with Dad deciding to buy a house of our own; I think Mum in particular had always preferred a house of her own, rather than a police one. Our new home was called Chynance, and it was right on the seafront at Portreath. There were no properties in front of us – we looked straight out onto the sea.

This also meant a return to Tolgus Secondary Modern School, which went along fine, until . . . another rugby match, and this time with me representing Tolgus against Camborne. Hence another "pummelling" for me, except that it was the other way round now, of course.

This apart, as I say, everything was still going fine for me, and in the process I was adding to my "gang" of pals. These included David Laity's brother Roddy, Andrew Harry (who died tragically in a motor accident just outside Portreath in 1974), Alan Roberts, brothers Andrew and Neil Sowter,

"Bonzo" Johns, son of the legendary Cornish rugby player of the same name, and Richard Pascoe, who I still see at every Redruth home match today.

There was a new interest for me when I reached the age of 14, as that qualified me to join the Portreath Surf Lifesaving Club – which is what most of my "gang" promptly did once we'd reached that birthday. We used to train every Tuesday, no matter what the weather. We did this all year round – with no wetsuits! We would spend a good hour in that sea, and thought nothing of it. Wetsuits were still very much in their infancy then and only "rich" people had them. We just wore our trunks, skull cap and belt.

During one training session, I was sent out on a ski to stand off the beach – about 300 yards out to sea – and when I was told to come back in I quickly realised that I was in difficulties. Quite simply, the tide was taking me out faster than I could walk in. In no time at all, I was heading for Gull Rock. Fortunately, those on the shore saw what was happening and two of the older lads from the club came out and put a reel belt around the ski and hauled me in.

It was dark and cold, it all seemed like a bit touch and go, and for me it was a frankly scary experience! I didn't actually panic. I knew they had spotted my predicament. All the same, it was a useful reminder to me of just how easily swimmers could get into difficulty, and it was very easy to see how someone in that situation WOULD panic.

At about this time – shortly after my 14th birthday – I got myself a part-time job as a window cleaner for an American businessman in Portreath. He owned the Portreath Treasure Trove, which comprised a café and, next door, a souvenir shop. The windows were gigantic, and I used to clean the entire collection, in both premises, for the princely sum of 20 pence. This work took about an hour. So I guess I could have re-written the definition for "slave labour."

After the main event, if I was lucky, I was allowed to add to my earnings by cleaning this guy's car as well. That doubled my money to 40 pence, and I really thought I was doing well. I can see now that I was definitely being exploited (I can't even write that 40 pence "was a lot of money in those days!") Nonetheless, I saved up all those 20 pences to go on a cruise! Or rather, it became the pocket money for that cruise.

It came during my final schooldays, joining my parents on board the SS Nevassa for 14 days to and in the Mediterranean. We went ashore in

Yugoslavia and the Greek islands, although a number of scheduled port calls were cancelled because Greece and Cyprus were at war with each other at the time. As well as washing windows and a car, I had also saved for this by cutting the grass of a family friend. Each time I did this, I got 50 pence – which was definitely a bit more like it!

My Grandparents, James and Ada Maloney.
James 1876-1956, Ada 1892-1929.

My Dad, James, circa 1945

My Dad, circa 1954

Mum and Dad with my daughter Clare, 1989

Dad, 1975

Colton School, 1964. I'm second from right, middle row.

Austhorpe School, 1968. I'm third from right in black jumper. The teacher is Mr Foxcroft. Others, left to right: Martin Carthy, Chris Corbage, unrecalled, unrecalled, Angela ------.

Centre of attention. Me celebrating promotion to Postman Higher Grade (PHG), at Blackheath, London, 1979.

44

Linda, my first wife, with baby Clare, 1989

Proud grandparents. Mum and Dad with Clare
at Greenwich Hospital, May 25, 1989.

CHAPTER FIVE

I BECOME ONE OF BRITAIN'S LAST TELEGRAM BOYS

During my last year at the Tolgus school – 1973-74 – I had been additionally studying to become an electrical engineer with the South Western Electricity Board (SWEB). I had a private tutor, Tommy Paull, who was a top engineer with the company and he was a great mathematician. He and his wife Rose were very good friends with my mum and dad.

At that time, there were only two new vacancies for apprentices with SWEB every year, so I knew I was going to be really up against it. I was also none too happy about having to stay at home in the evenings for all this private tuition – when what I really wanted to be doing was playing football outside with my mates.

Then one evening I was sat at home reading the *West Briton* newspaper when I saw an advert in the jobs section that was to change my direction and outlook altogether and lead to a big phase of my early working life. The advert was for a telegram boy with the GPO. From the job description, I couldn't help thinking that this was precisely the sort of thing that would suit me. It emphasised the outdoor nature of the work – meeting different types of people and riding motor bikes, plus their support, and facilities, for sports activities. They even had their own football team. The pay was £13 a week, as opposed to £8 for a SWEB apprentice.

I had already concluded that I was not university material – in fact, I'm not at all sure I would have wanted to go that way even if I was up to it – and I told my parents this was the job I wanted to go after. Mum and Dad were both against the idea, but I was so keen on it that nothing was going to stop me! They eventually came round to my way of thinking and I found myself heading for Redruth Post Office for an interview.

There were a dozen of us there in all, competing for that job, and I was the only one from Tolgus; the rest were all from Grammar School. We all got called in to do an exam, which included English and Maths, and then had to wait outside while our papers were assessed. Then, one by one, we were called back in to see the examining panel of three people – the postmaster and two inspectors. I was the last to be called in and I thought: "I haven't got a hope in hell against these people; they're all from Grammar School."

The panellists asked me lots of questions. It turned out one of them was a keen cricketer and, detecting my Yorkshire accent, he asked me what I thought of Yorkshire cricket. I was not exactly hot on cricket, so I bungled my way through the answer. I stressed that I was very keen on sport generally and loved the outdoor life. Then I had to go back outside for another half-hour. To my great surprise, when they asked me to return, I was told that I had got the job. Cue jubilation.

Alas, this was my first "proper job" – but I ended up never actually working from Redruth Post Office. The reason – can you guess? – is that my family were on the move yet again! Yet another new life lay ahead for me. This time we were bound for Reading – to Thatcham, to be precise, in Berkshire. Dad's job was behind it again, and by now he had been promoted to sergeant. He kept that lovely new house of ours in Portreath, renting it out, and he later returned there with Mum to retire.

And what a dump Thatcham was after Cornwall. Our latest residence was No 3, Longcroft Road, a police property rented from the local council. I didn't like it and nor did my sister Caroline, poor girl. I remember seeing her sitting on a low wall opposite our front gate and she was crying her heart out. She loved Cornwall so much, and this was sheer torture for her. My heart went out to her.

I personally took the view that we were here now and so we might as well try and make the most of it. For starters, we had better get to know the locals, and all in all they were quite nice people – except, would you believe, our next door neighbours – the "neighbours from hell," as I dubbed them. It soon became clear that they hated the police, full stop. In Leeds and Cornwall, Mum and Dad had never experienced any anti-police abuse, and nor had I, so this was something completely new to us. The verbal abuse, as my parents arrived home or left, was quite something and several times resulted in other police officers being called to the scene. These neighbours were truly horrible people. The law clearly meant nothing to them; it seemed they had no respect for anyone or anything.

In August, 1974, I experienced something of a culture shock as I began my work based at Reading Post Office, having had a transfer from Cornwall. This headquarters building was massive – really quite intimidating - and I was a 5ft 2in "boy" in a 6ft 2in man's world! I was, in fact, one of the last telegram boys in the country, with something of a revolution in technology and communications not too far away now.

I was awestruck, but also very excited. Furthermore, although I didn't know it yet, it was the first day of a roller-coaster life for me; it would lead to my travelling all over the world. I was fitted out for my uniform and given my badge number, which I have always remembered – 272. That was my identification all through my postal life.

Before I hit the road for real, we had to train on all sorts of postal duties first (bearing in mind that I could remain a telegram boy for only so long, prior to upgrading to full postman duties). I remember being put onto what was known as "rebate mail" – or junk mail, as it is more commonly known. This was the worst because it weighed a ton. For my very first delivery, I'm convinced that bag weighed more than I did!

I became really good mates with a guy called Dennis Waters who started on the same day as I did. He was much bigger than I was and he was also a bit of an opportunist. For ten pence a time, he agreed to carry my bag as well as his own. So off we would go on our round together, with him carrying two bags. I would run up and down the driveways delivering the individual items of mail from the big bag. Dennis and I would always be the first to finish, and they couldn't work out why! We worked a good system that served both of us well in our own ways – what a team! We stayed good friends and even became trade union representatives together. We became the scourge of the wages department. Whenever anyone received incorrect wages, off we would go, straightaway, to put matters right.

When the time came for me to start my training on a moped (my mode of transport for delivering telegrams, as I was too small for a proper motor bike), it was touch and go whether my feet could reach the ground, as I was so short. They did, just. Everyone said I would never pass my moped test, but Steve Landon, my immediate boss, in charge of the telegrams department, always had confidence in me.

So for weeks on end I studied the Highway Code and my mum in particular was mightily impressed. Came the day of my test and thus my introduction to Mr Jennings, the adjudicator, a man with whom I would cross swords a number of times in the years to come. He outlined the route he wanted me to take from Reading Post Office and he would follow on his own motor bike. Only trouble was, half way along this course, I lost him! I took a wrong turning. I returned to the Post Office and waited for what I thought would be a right bollocking, but he was okay about it and just told me again where he wanted me to go.

So off we went once more, only for an action replay! Half-way into it, my memory went and the remainder of the route was lost to me. I was given one more chance – with the clear warning that if I fluffed the route this time that would be it, I would have failed. "I have other people to test," he helpfully pointed out. Well, I didn't fluff my final chance, and I have never known such a feeling of elation. Half the candidates failed – and they were just put onto normal post or sorting duties, whereas I was now basking in the pride and prestige of my new status as a telegram boy.

My new role opened doors, you could say, to the rich and famous, with mixed experiences. The big names that spring to mind are Dave Allen, who used to live at Woodcote in Berkshire, George Harrison (Henley), Lyn Paull (Stratfield Saye), and Danny La Rue (who owned a pub at Goring-on-Thames).

First time round with Dave Allen, I actually delivered to the wrong house! There was a barn at the end of the drive, but it looked to me like a big house, big enough to be the great man's residence, I figured. I knocked on the door, but got no answer. So I put the telegram through the letterbox. When I returned to base, I was called into the inspector's office and told in no uncertain terms of my mistake. (Some telegrams needed signing for, but others didn't and this one fell into the latter category.)

Next time I delivered to Dave Allen, I actually met him and duly apologised. He made a joke about it and immediately put me at my ease. In all, I must have delivered to him some 20 times over some two years; there were no mobile phones, fax or internet then, so telegrams were the fastest way of communicating in writing.

I suppose Dave Allen's comedy style was what would be classified as "edgy" today, and because of that a lot of people didn't like him, but I found him a really nice, polite guy – albeit with tell-tale signs that he was fond, as per his screen image, of a drink or two. He was one of my very first customers and we would usually have a chat – over a cup of tea! I would just drive right up to his door – something which I guess would no longer be possible in today's high-security age.

When visiting George Harrison, I came a cropper one April when there had been a late snowfall. It was lying some four inches deep on the ground and I got off my moped to open the gates of Catcombe Park. Unfortunately, the snow was so thick that you could no longer tell exactly where the grass verges bordered the driveway. All of a sudden, I found myself separated from my machine and lying on my back in that snow! I had struck the verge and fallen off. I was well-padded, and so I was relatively unscathed and able to pick myself up again quickly. I put the moped on its stand and walked the remaining 200 yards to the Beatle's door.

There was no bell, just a great big brass knocker on the wooden door. I banged on that door as loud as I could and then stood back, hoping to meet the great man and ask for his autograph. Instead, and after what seemed like a lifetime of waiting, the door opened and I was greeted by a maid – or it may have been the cleaner.

Deflated, I meekly announced: "I've got a telegram for Mr Harrison." "Okay, I'll take that for him," she said. But I insisted: "He has to sign for it himself." Good try, but it didn't work. I was so disappointed. I trudged away in the snow with an autograph – of the housemaid or cleaner. I returned to George's house with telegrams many more times and I even got to meet him two or three times. He never had a lot to say; he was just courteous and politely mentioned the weather and asked how far I had come. It was only ever doorstep stuff; he never invited me in. And I never did get his autograph. Each time I went there, I would tell myself: "This is it; this time I will get it." But I always bottled out. You know when you can ask and when you can't. My time with George Harrison never came.

Lyn Paull lived in the village of Stratfield Saye in Hampshire. It was a beautiful spring morning when I made my one and only trip there. The sun was still rising and, after I had rung her doorbell, the lady herself put her head out from the bedroom window above. I was satisfied beyond reasonable doubt that she was naked at that moment. I said: "Telegram, Miss Paull." She replied: "Okay, won't be a minute."

Anticipation levels soared. So you can imagine my deflation, again, when the door opened and a man, wearing just his dressing gown, emerged. "I'll give that to Miss Paull," he said. "Thanks," I croaked. I was gutted, and trooped off once more in disconsolate fashion. But at least I'd seen her and spoken to her!

Danny La Rue was a lovely man, although I also recall that he never seemed to be a well man. As with George Harrison, I must have delivered to his pub more than 20 times. He was the perfect gentleman and sometimes he would take time out to sit down and have a coffee and chat with me. If the weather was nice, we would do this on the weir outside the pub; it was a beautiful setting. We would discuss life in general and comedy in particular. I told him how I had met up with Dave Allen, and he knew Dave, of course.

CHAPTER SIX

THE REAL THING - MY FIRST
SIGHTING OF A NAKED LADY!

My days at Reading introduced me to a new set of friends – and my first sighting of a naked lady. This was followed, for good measure, by my second naked lady sighting, which was in even more bizarre circumstances than the first.

As well as my excellent mate Dennis Waters, I also acquired good pals in Graham Turner, Les Little and Kevin (surname forgotten), whose parents owned a fish tackle shop in Reading. Martin Clarke was one of the older lads, while there was also a huge man – in height and roundness – whose proper name I never did find out. Everyone just called him Dog. He would have been great playing rugby; instead, he played for the works soccer team.

These were all good guys, but I also had to work with a dead miserable guy by the name, perhaps appropriately, of Mr Grubb. He wasn't actually obnoxious, but he had a very dry sense of humour, and always came across as just such a miserable bugger!

My typical working day began around 10 am and finished about seven hours later. You could play cards and sit around with coffee and cans of Coke . . . or there would be days when it was a constant race against the clock. It was just a question of responding to whatever demand arose. On my little moped I had to cover a pretty wide area, in all weathers, at the tender age of 16. My area took in Berkshire, Oxfordshire and parts of Hampshire.

Thus it was that I joined the Post Office and saw . . . not exactly the world, but at least my first naked lady! I had to deliver a telegram to a house on the main road down to Basingstoke. It wasn't to anyone famous. The door opened and, to my great shock – and delight – there she was in all her naked glory. She was in her 40s, I guess, very attractive, with a nice figure and long auburn hair . . . standing totally starkers, and expressionless, in her doorway. In as normal a tone as I could muster, I told her: "I have a telegram for you." Her face didn't change. She just said "thank you very much" and shut the door again. It was just as if this was the sort of thing she did every day. Maybe it was! I turned and went. Some images remain very vivid in your mind for the rest of your life. This was definitely one of them for me!

A few weeks later I was rubbing my eyes in disbelief once again . . . and beginning to wonder whether Reading was full of naked women on public display! I was in the city centre area on my moped when I pulled up at the traffic lights alongside a Morris 1000. I idly glanced down into that car, to be met by the amazing sight of a woman – in her 50s, I'd say – sat in the back seat, with not a stitch of clothing on her body! She caught me looking at her, at which point I looked away. But I couldn't resist looking again, of course, and there she still was – I hadn't imagined it! This time, she just continued staring ahead, expressionless, until the lights changed and the car drove off. Amazing or what? But definitely true!

There were telegrams and telegrams. To deliver those with wedding congratulations was fantastic. It meant everyone was incredibly happy and we would get invited inside to join the party for a moment and have a drink. That was not strictly speaking allowed, of course, but . . . On the outskirts of Reading, where the better-off lived, we would come across large marquees and no-expense-spared types of receptions, with terrific party atmospheres.

Alas, every silver lining has a dark cloud and the part of my job that I hated most, as you can guess, was the telegram bringing news of a death. I must have delivered hundreds of these. We were instructed that we should just hand them over and walk away, but I could never do that. I knew what these telegrams conveyed and I would say: "Would you like to sit down? I'm afraid I have some very bad news for you." Nine times out of ten the recipient knew what it was, and even who it was who had died.

On other occasions, it would come as a complete shock. In that case, I would reinforce the suggestion that I come inside and sit down with them. Some people even passed out on reading this sort of telegram (although mercifully this never happened with me). I would stay with them until they were okay – or at least until they had given me a phone number for me to contact a relative or friend for them. This was always a heart-breaking experience; it was the only part of the job that I genuinely disliked. I hated it.

In 1975, I was invited to be a steward at the Reading Festival, which was then in its infancy. The promoters would come to the Post Office and ask for volunteers, which so far as I was concerned was great. It was a good weekend and a good experience for me, although I suspect it was also a good deal more peaceful than it has become; it was a very "hippy" sort of thing then. I don't even recall any rain or mud, which was unusual for pop concerts.

In the same year, I was also a steward for the Henley Regatta, which was a bit more of a snobbish affair, definitely not the sort of thing I would volunteer for again. People would completely ignore us, even though we were being paid for our services; they would treat you like dirt. Most of the people there were just so far up their own backsides, it wasn't true. I was glad to have gained the experience, but it wasn't an enjoyable one.

I managed to get picked for the Reading Post Office football team – on the right wing as always. The division we played in also had teams from the police, army – and a prison. The latter obviously could not play away matches and so we played two games every season at this prison. The opposition here never fielded anything like the same line-up twice, with inmates constantly on the move, just starting or just finishing their time. They were always very fit, though, and a striking memory is of their football field being lined all round with prison guards. We were always made very welcome, and there were never any fisticuffs.

Still with sport, I discovered there was a big betting culture in the Post Office. They were all constantly having a little bet in some way or other; it seemed everyone had a newspaper stuck in their back pocket. I duly joined in. I would have a ten pence bet every now and again (I was earning £13.60 a week after all!) I even came up trumps when I collected all of £20 after backing a 200-1 horse. It was the last one in the list and, whether I was feeling sorry for it or what, I put my money on it and it romped home, earning me one-and-a-half weeks' wages!

During my time at Reading, the IRA's attacks on mainland Britain were at their peak, and this was one of the reasons my dad was transferred to Reading – to help combat the IRA threat. I didn't realise it at the time, but this also involved "feathermen" being designated to look after the families of the policemen. Most of these guys had some kind of special forces training, and they did their work for the families of the Army as well as the police. We were deemed to be at high risk.

I remember finishing my work early one lunchtime and walking across the road in the direction of the main Reading train station. For some reason, I stopped and looked in a sales window with motor bikes on display. In the window reflection, I suddenly noticed a man looking directly at me. So I moved away from the direction of the station – but he stayed with me, still looking at me. I thought he must have been some sort of nutcase, but when I told my dad this he just said not to worry and explained about the "feathermen," watching over us to make sure we were okay.

My awareness of the IRA was further strengthened one day when I returned to Reading Post Office and made straight for a lift. I joined two postmen who were chaperoning a large black box. They explained that it contained a suspected letter bomb and it was being taken down to the basement, where they had sandbags and so on to deal with this sort of thing. It turned out to be a false alarm, but that was the longest lift descent I have ever known, I can tell you. It seemed to take forever. By now, I was no longer in any doubt that the IRA posed a very real threat, close at hand.

One of the postmen based at Reading was Irish – or a "mad Irishman", as we fondly thought of him. Not knowing any better, I jokingly asked "is that a bomb you've got there, mate?" as I passed him on the stairs, with a parcel in his hands. He did not regard that as remotely funny, chasing me all over the building and unleashing a tirade of expletives. I managed to shake him off, but it was a lesson well learned. I was only 18, and simply hadn't realised what I had said. In fairness to this guy, he later joined us in the telegram department, and turned out to be perfectly okay with me.

I was a busy bee at Reading. As well as doing the job, and playing for the football team, I had also become a trade union representative, starting at the tender age of 16. About six months into that, however, the guy who had been instrumental in landing me this position was sacked after being discovered having sex with a canteen worker in the back of a Post Office van. Someone reported that the van was "rocking" and a police officer turned up, opened the door and discovered them at it. His sacking upset me and shook us all (there were some 400 of us working at Reading Post

Office). He was a really well respected guy, well liked by everyone, and had been a union rep himself for many years, including local branch chairman. He knew his union business inside out and came across as very much a family man; he certainly had that fatherly touch towards me, and his sacking left me gutted, to be honest.

My job as a telegram boy also led to my first visit to London – albeit not in quite the way intended. I used to catch the 1038 train every morning from Thatcham to Reading, a journey of about 17 minutes. The Thatcham "station" was just a platform, with no ticket barrier or any staff. The train was a two- or three-carriage affair – normally.

On the train itself, I got pally with the regular guard. I used to sit with him in the guard's room and chat our way into Reading. One morning, I was standing on the platform, waiting as usual, when in pulled a great big express train. I thought this was a little strange, but everyone on the platform got onto it, so I followed suit, thinking that maybe the regular train had broken down.

We stopped at Reading West and then, just after it had started up again, I got out of my seat in readiness for getting off at the main Reading station. Instead, I couldn't help noticing that the train was gathering speed; I looked out of the window and saw that we were on the middle track. Sure enough, the train just shot through Reading without stopping. I thought: "Blimey, I'm going to be late for work; that's a written warning."

I ended up in Paddington Station. I jumped off the train and made for the first public phone box I set eyes on. I told my colleagues what had happened and got onto the next train back. I explained to the guard – not my pal – what had happened, and he let me back to Reading for no charge. I arrived in work two hours late and, mercifully, my explanation was accepted and I escaped without a written warning.

All told, I had 20 great months at Reading and I reflected that I had arrived there as a boy and left as a man. It was indeed time for another move, with my Dad being transferred in his work again, and with the IRA once more having a direct influence on my life.

CHAPTER SEVEN

MY ENCOUNTERS WITH YOBS AND 'ATTILLA THE HUN'

My Dad was transferred to Woolwich in South London as a direct result of the IRA bombing the barracks there and a nearby pub, the Kings Arms (which is now a landmark on the route of the London Marathon). Two people were killed in the pub explosion; three soldiers were injured at the barracks.

For my own transfer to Woolwich Post Office, I was met at the telegram office by one of my two bosses, Jim Gosling. He was a really nice guy who made me feel very welcome straightaway, as did my fellow telegram boys. I had been very lucky in that this was my third post office in less than two years and I had only come across nice people. The big wide world that everyone said would scare me had so far been very kind.

That changed at lunchtime on my first day of work in Woolwich. I encountered Attilla the Hun in the form of a Mr Staples, my other manager – or "Paper Clip" as he was known to all of us. He didn't even have the courtesy to shake my hand. Rather than joining in the welcomes, he came out with a series of insults to me – "country bumpkin" etc.

Okay, I thought, I've just met my first prat between Cornwall and London. But there's no denying I was shocked – I was not expecting this from a man in his 60s. The lads told me just to ignore him – so at least they weren't going to jump on his bandwagon and give me problems. In time I learnt that Attilla had heard about my status as an up-and-coming union rep and wanted to "put me in my place."

He clearly had it in for me right from the start. He gave me the oldest moped you had ever seen. I had in fact progressed to motor bikes by now, so I supposed this was all part of Attilla's hard-time plan for me. It must have been one of the very first mopeds that ever came out; you could have walked faster.

In Woolwich, the hill from the train station to the barracks is one of the steepest and longest – must be a good mile - in London. Attilla gave me a telegram to deliver to an address at the top of this hill. That moped was never going to make it. So I parked it half-way up and walked the rest of the way! It was a lot quicker. I was back in the office in a few minutes – not breathless or anything – and Attilla demanded to know why I had been so quick and "where I had put the telegram."

I said: "The bike just flew up that hill!" But I was too clever for my own good. He responded: "In that case, that moped is yours from now on." So I was stuck with that old heap in the afternoons. I was okay on the morning shifts, because Jim Gosling was my manager then and he saw to it that I had a motor bike. I could have complained about Attilla's treatment of me – either through my union or to my bosses higher up the line – but I felt that I wasn't going to give this guy that satisfaction. So I stuck with the moped in the afternoons – but delivered precious few telegrams then because it took me so long to get everywhere.

Throughout my time at Woolwich, there was constant awkwardness between me and this guy, but I did my best not to let him see how it was getting to me. Plus, any really difficult jobs were very kindly taken over by my colleagues anyway, without Attilla knowing, of course.

I only had to endure this treatment for two short months, because in May 1976 I was starting all over again, this time at Abbeywood, in London, following Dad's transfer there. And this time we couldn't have been blessed with nicer neighbours. Well, they were fellow police officers – Arthur and Sadie Aitcheson – and I learned that Dad had joined the force the very same day as Arthur had done. Both had since been around the country and now here they were together again, some 25 years later, back where they first met and joined.

As for me now, I was still a telegram boy, being just a few months off my 18th birthday. Unfortunately, I had only been in my new job for a fortnight when I became a crime victim. I had got friendly with my new colleagues and they had asked me to join them for a drink one evening. To get to the pub, I had to cross a couple of football pitches to reach a bus stop. I was running across one of these fields one dark evening when all of a sudden I was hit square in the face by something. It knocked me to the ground, and it turned out I was being mugged.

Three yobs had set upon me. I was stunned – there had been no warning of any kind – but I managed to pull myself together after a minute or so and realise what was going on. They were telling me to pull my pockets out because they wanted my money. Luckily for me, a man nearby heard the commotion and between the two of us we managed to see them off. The man brought me into his house, sat me down and phoned my mum and dad.

They called the police – who knew exactly who the culprits were, from the descriptions I was able to give them. They were well known to the police and they were arrested. They went to court and, I believe, were given community orders or something similar. They pleaded guilty, so I did not need to attend. They hadn't actually managed to take anything from me – but I didn't get that night out with the lads!

I encountered more trouble a few months later when an old friend of Mum's from Berwick-on-Tweed came down for something of a reunion, and I was sent out to get some lemonade so that they could enjoy their whisky and lemonade tipples. The off-licence was about a quarter of a mile away and I still had my slippers on.

As I approached the off-licence, I saw 20 to 30 youths – boys and girls – gathered outside. They included the three who had gone to court after attacking me. They recognised me and began shouting abuse and threats. I made my way through them and into the building, where a woman behind the counter told me to lock the door as the situation was "getting nasty." But it was too late – they were already in. I had bought my bottle of lemonade, so I made my way out again and began walking home.

I thought that was the end of the matter, but when I was about half-way back all hell broke loose. This gang were chasing after me and ended up surrounding me. A woman passer-by saw what was happening, recognised me and went to a police house for help. Arthur Aitcheson arrived on the scene. He was a big man and he threatened them with arrest, but he was outnumbered and these youths now laid into him. Then my father arrived, but he, too, was set upon.

I had managed to get away, but I was then chased up the road by a yob in his late 20s. I stopped running and turned to face him, head on. I knew running away was wrong, so I just dropped the bottle on the grass. I went for this moron and he fell over a small border fence, about nine inches high. I picked up the bottle and went back to where my Dad and Arthur had been overpowered by those moronic scum. I went for a blonde head, which belonged to the ring leader, who was raining kicks and punches at my Dad. I hit him with the lemonade bottle. The bottle shattered – but astonishingly, with no apparent effect on this slimeball. What's that they say – "no sense, no feeling?" I was left holding the neck of the bottle - I might just as well have hit him with a rolled-up newspaper. At that stage, I really thought that was it – they would kill me; but just at that moment police reinforcements – cars and vans – arrived. It was a fair old riot.

Even more amazingly, even though this gang of thugs were clearly the perpetrators of all the trouble, they actually made complaints against ME! The next day, police officers came around to my home to follow up the complaints! They explained that they had no choice but to arrest me and I was charged with assault! I told my bosses at work and they came to court on the day of my trial. If I had been found guilty, that would have been the end of my career with the Post Office.

The foreman of the jury returned the verdict – NOT GUILTY – and I could have kissed that lady. Despite their battering, my dad and Arthur suffered no serious injuries and I had escaped with just some bruises. But the whole thing – incidents and court case – had been a very scary experience. It was my first taste of the dark side of London – I'd never known anything like it before – and I felt I had grown up in a very short space of time. In a separate court case, the three ring leaders were sent to prison, and fortunately for me I never encountered any more trouble like that.

CHAPTER EIGHT

GETTING TO KNOW SOME OF THE 'RICH AND FAMOUS'

All good things come to an end and by definition my days as a telegram boy were strictly numbered. It seems incredible now, in this age of superfast communications over the internet, mobile phones and so on, that GPO telegrams were once the quickest way to send an important message. In its hey day, in the 1930s, the service was delivering an average of 65 million telegrams a year. By 1976, that figure had dropped to just 844 and a year later the Post Office took the decision to abolish the service.

I enjoyed my time as a telegram boy; in fact, I loved it. The life was good and it wasn't exactly hard. I don't think I realised it at the time, but I was well looked after. My superiors, by and large, made a special effort to make sure that I was okay and coming along, progressing well.

But of course my age brought my own role as a telegram boy to an end, and I wanted to "climb the ladder" anyway. So in 1976 I was on the move once more, this time taking up my first job as an ordinary postman, albeit at my fourth office, namely Blackheath, where I worked until 1982, with more good friends made in the process.

On my first day in my new job there, I was introduced to the office inspector, a charming man whose name eludes me. Things were very different in those days, not least in the system of ranks, which was a bit on a par with those of the Police Force. We had a postman, then a postman highergrade (equivalent to a sergeant), and then assistant inspector, inspector, chief inspector and superintendent. (This hierarchy has long since gone out the window.)

As I left the inspector's office on my first morning at Blackheath, I was handed over to a postman who was to become a great pal of mine, Jim Stevens, who was nicknamed "Jethro" (after Jethro Tull, the British rock singer, because he looked like him - not the Cornish comedian). He showed me around all the offices, which were almost empty as nearly everyone was out delivering. Although I didn't know it then, Jethro and I were to become lifelong close friends. He became like an older brother to me; e even came down to Cornwall later on to meet my mum and dad.

But on that first day of mine at Blackheath, as "Jethro" was showing me around, I had a memorable first encounter with one of my new colleagues. We were walking along a corridor towards the inspector's office when I saw a great big guy – who I can only describe as a human brick shithouse! – striding towards me. This was one George Sedden, a Scouser ex-Royal Marine – a massive man, with a big black beard. (Think Bluto in the old Popeye cartoons!) Jethro introduced him to me and, with no warning, Brick Shithouse aimed a great globule of spit all over the lapel of my uniform!

I was stunned and it took me a few seconds for me to realise what he had just done. Then it dawned on me. The spit had been aimed directly, and accurately, at my Leeds United badge. I used to wear lapel badges (the other one being my union badge). I saw red and, without thinking and despite the fact that he was seemingly twice as big as I was, I just punched him in the face with all the force that my 5ft 4in frame could muster. It was a beauty of a punch, although I say it myself, and yet all that transpired was the feeling that I had broken my hand. Brick Shithouse just stood there with a big smile on his face – at which point my own incredulous expression must have been quite a picture!

He hadn't even flinched. Then he held out his hand and said: "Welcome to Blackheath. Are you coming for a pint?" So George, who was a staunch Liverpool supporter, duly became another of my friends. What a character he was. I remember the first time I went round to his house. His wife answered the door and said yes, he was in. She ushered me into the lounge – where George, in all his naked glory, was washing himself in an old metal bath in the middle of the room. He didn't care; he just carried on with his bath, chatting away to me, as down to earth as they come and not batting an eyelid. (They lived in an old house, with no bathroom.) It was all just so normal to George – but it amazed me.

We became good drinking buddies. If we did a double shift, we would have a break of one-and-a-half hours and we would go to George's local in Blackheath, the Royal Oak. I would watch him and some of the lads playing crib – which I could never play myself. We also travelled around together to sports matches. He came with me to see Leeds beat St Helens by 14-12 in the Rugby Challenge Cup Final at Wembley in 1978. (George was a fanatical St Helens supporter, whereas I came from Leeds, of course; need I say more!)

There was an amusing sequel to one pub visit when I gave a lift to George and another postman, Martin Kearney, in one of the old J4 vans with the sliding doors. In these vans, the engine was in the middle, between the two seats, and so one passenger could sit in the proper seat and the other could sit on top of the engine casing. As I drove round a corner, George was sitting on the engine and Martin in the passenger seat. The momentum swung George to his left side and Martin (who was later to become a police officer in the RAF), ended up falling out of the van and performing several somersaults along the roadside.

Amazingly, he wasn't hurt – but he was a big, strong lad. We quickly came to a halt and George and I could scarcely stop laughing. We had, of course, all been drinking, and if the police had come along we, or at least I as the driver, would have been in trouble. But we got away with it. I'm not condoning what we did, but just pointing out that in those days drink-driving still wasn't the issue it has long since become.

During my time at Blackheath – one of the more prosperous areas of London – I met a number of famous people. As well as work, though, I also met a couple of "big names" in the world of sport – the late, great Jock Stein and Alex Sabella, who, as I write now, is the current coach of the Argentina national soccer team.

Jock was manager of my beloved Leeds United for all of 45 days in 1978, coming down south of the border after enormous success with Celtic but then resigning to take up the post of manager of Scotland. I was there with Jethro, at Elland Road, for his first match in charge, an evening fixture with Manchester United.

We got into the stadium early and were sitting in our seats in the West Stand, with pints and pies, when we saw the great man emerge onto the pitch. We raced down to the side of the pitch and asked him for his autograph, which he readily gave. He signed my match day programme, which, of course, I have kept to this day. We didn't talk as such. I just said: "Jock, could you sign this, please?" I didn't need to go on to the pitch. There was just a low boundary wall which we could stretch across, and he was close by.

Leeds were also playing Manchester United when I got Alex Sabella's autograph. This was in 1980 and Alex was playing in midfield for Leeds. I remember he was extremely smart pre-match, wearing a beautiful medium-green suit. He made 23 appearances for my team, having moved there from Sheffield United – who had first tried to sign Diego Maradona! As I write, I think Argentina are still unbeaten under his leadership, which began in 2011.

Big names I met during my rounds as a postman in Blackheath included Stephen Lewis, who was Blakey in the TV series "On The Buses." I was actually his postman for a long time and he was a lovely fellow. I remember he owned one of those quaint old three-wheeler Robin Reliant cars. He was a very quiet, unassuming sort of guy.

Then there was Terry Waite, who, as envoy for the Church of England, travelled to Lebanon to try to secure the release of four hostages and was himself held captive between 1987 and 1991. I saw him nearly every day. This was chiefly because he had to sign so many Recorded Delivery documents in relation to parking tickets he had picked up! Presumably, in his diplomat's role for the church, he would have had these waived. He, too, was a very down-to-earth person and very polite – another lovely fellow. He lived in a Victorian semi-detached house, just off Tranquil Vale and opposite the Three Tuns public house.

When I was on the parcel run, I would deliver to Jim Davidson when he was still an up-and-coming comedian. It was very clear to me, even then, that he was definitely bound for the very top. At that time, he was just doing the pubs and clubs scene. As well as meeting him in my work, I would go along to see him entertaining, and he was tremendously funny. Sad to say, I don't like his stuff these days; it has become altogether too smutty for my taste.

And someone I didn't take to at all was Jim Callaghan, the former Labour leader whose post I delivered in the days before he became Prime Minister. He took over from Harold Wilson in 1976 but was beaten by Margaret Thatcher in the 1979 General Election. He lived next door to the singer Kate Bush. I met him a few times but he was not even courteous, let alone friendly. He seemed very full of himself and would just sign things and stuff them back into my hand without any pleasantries, implying that I was some sort of low life that he couldn't stoop to deal with.

I only met Kate Bush once (she was usually away), but we had a couple of minutes' chat and she struck me as a really nice young lady. I didn't get her autograph – it was not really the done thing for a postman! Her eclectic musical style and idiosyncratic vocal style made her one of the UK's most successful solo female performers of the past 40 years.

Another famous name I got to know in Blackheath (yes, becoming a bit like a Who's Who, this, isn't it!) was Omar Sharif, no less, the Egyptian actor who has starred in such all-time Hollywood greats as "Lawrence of Arabia", "Doctor Zhivago" and "Funny Girl."

Omar was not a local resident himself, but he had friends who lived in Blackheath Park – it was a bit of a Millionaires Row for the rich and famous. I quite often spoke to Omar, who would stay up all night playing bridge. When I delivered in the morning, he would still be sitting there and would invite me to join him in a cup of coffee before he went to bed. I wouldn't always have time for that coffee – but accepted his kind offer as often as I could! He tried to talk to me about bridge, but that was beyond me; I could not understand it. He would give me a sly smile, which left me in no doubt that he appreciated that fact! We must have sat down together 20 or more times; he took a genuine interest in my job and the other people I met on my rounds.

Then there was Max Wall, the English comedian and actor whose long performing career covered music hall, theatre, films and TV. (He died tragically in 1990, when he fell at Simpson's Restaurant in central London, fracturing his skull and never regaining consciousness.)

He lived just round the corner from Terry Waite and became a good friend. He loved our company – mine and Jethro's. His tipple was a pint of Guinness, and our friendship began when he just came over to us one day in the Three Tuns. He asked if he could join us – we knew who he was, of course, but until then we hadn't actually been acquainted with each other.

Max was one of the old-school comedians. He was very warm-hearted and I remember he always wore a duffle coat. One day he looked at my drink and asked: "What's that?" "Delicious!" I replied. He liked that answer. I've used it often since ("if it's good enough for Max Wall . . . ") and for all I know the great man may have used it himself.

My "less friendly" file, meanwhile, also includes Glenda Jackson, the former actress turned British Labour MP. She lived just down the road from Jim Davidson's parents (which is where Jim was living, as opposed to a home of his own then) and there was a postbox just outside her house where I collected from two or three times every day.

I saw her quite often, but I wasn't overly struck by her. I found her a bit off-ish. In fact, to be honest, she was a bit obnoxious – another of those lofty, high-and-mighty types who didn't want to know about any conversation with you.

CHAPTER NINE

LIVELY SESSIONS WITH
BILLY CONNOLLY

Another famous man, or rather couple, that I met away from work were Billy Connolly and Pam Stephenson. This came about when three of us – myself, Jethro and another postman pal, Billy Rutter – were in the indoor arena at the old Wembley watching a national five-a-side soccer tournament. This was held every year and involved around 30 teams. It went on all day and provided great entertainment.

We were sat there with our pints of beer, watching the warm-up, before it all started, when Jethro suddenly said "listen," indicating the voices of the people behind us. We looked around and realised that it was none other than Billy and Pam. Billy looked at us and said "Hello, lads." We replied: "Hello, Billy." We got to know him quite well, chatting away and passing the drinks backwards and forwards during the six or seven hours we were there.

At the end of that day's entertainment, we said our goodbyes and adjourned to an Indian restaurant, where we congratulated ourselves on having got to know the great Billy Connolly – and thought no more of it. The next day, however, Jethro and I went to the Apollo Victoria, a big theatre near Victoria Square, to see the Alex Harvey Band (originally the Sensational Alex Harvey Band). We walked in, only to discover, dining at a table just inside, none other than Billy and Pam! We had no idea they would be there; it had never been mentioned between us the previous day. Talk about small world.

They were both tucking into their dishes of Jambalaya, and making a right mess of it, as you do. Billy looked up and said: "You two, you're following us?" "Blimey, Billy, no," we reassured him. We moved on to the bar, where Jethro and I discussed the possibility of getting Billy's autograph. We would have another pint and then decide.

We didn't need much persuasion, and in fact hatched a slightly more elaborate plan. We duly went back to their table and asked: "If we could get a photograph of you now, is there any chance we could send it to you for you to autograph and send back to us?" He said: "No problem, but you will have to find the photographer." That actually didn't appear too difficult, as the place was teeming with cameramen.

We found a freelancer from Manchester, but when we told him what we wanted he refused point blank. "I'm not going anywhere near that madman," he explained. We weren't ready to take no for an answer, though. We pressed, gave him £10 – a fiver from each of us – and he finally agreed. We went back to Billy's table and he took the photograph (of just Billy). I still have it – it is framed and usually hangs in my hallway.

Billy gave us his address and the photographer sent us six photos. We selected three of them and sent them off to Billy. We got them back, autographed as requested. For some reason I forget, we gave him the Blackheath sorting office as our address, rather than the private address of one of us.

And that caused a bit of a problem initially. One morning Jethro and I got called into the inspector's office – we didn't have a clue what for. The inspector held up a large buff envelope and said: "What's this?" It was addressed to the pair of us, care of the Blackheath sorting office. Jethro (who maybe should have been a comedian, like his Cornish namesake!) replied: "It's an envelope, Sir." "Don't be so funny," came back the crack. He wanted to know why it had been addressed to us here, which was strictly against the rules.

It was several months now since we had seen Billy, and we did not immediately twig. Then the penny dropped, we explained what it was all about, and the inspector was fine about it. I kept one of the photos and Jethro took the other two, with one going to one of his relations. I have since seen Billy Connolly three or four times in live concerts, but never again met him personally. But what happy memories he left us with. That afternoon at Wembley, the jokes flowed thick and fast. Quite a lot of people had difficulty in understanding Billy in those days, with his thick Glaswegian accent and rough-and-ready personality, but I had no trouble – he actually came from a part of Glasgow where some of my own family had lived. He loved the fact that my mother was a Scot; that went down very well.

I followed his career very closely – he is a fantastic actor – and there's no doubting that Pamela definitely changed him. He had a big drink problem in his early days, but that's long since been put all behind him.

Through Jethro, still during my time at Blackheath, I was also introduced to Tony Hoare, who was a BBC producer and a big fan of Laurel and Hardy. As Freemasons have their lodges, so do Laurel and Hardy fans have their "tents" (after an L & H film called "The Tent"). Tony belonged to the same tent as Jethro. He was the producer of "Blankety Blank" and Jethro and I got invited to see the making of two of those shows one evening.

We sat through them – finding them quite funny – and then went to the bar upstairs, where I was introduced to Tony. He married Lois Laurel, Stan's granddaughter, a year or so later, with a reception at Leigh Park in Blackheath. It was held in the house of Alistair Barnett, a wine merchant magnate (in the days when off-licences were to be found all over London and elsewhere). Alistair and his wife each owned a Rolls Royce, with personalised number plates; that's how wealthy they were. Jethro and I were invited to the evening celebrations. That evening, we met a great many people from the TV world – not star screen names but more behind-the-scenes people like Tony Hoare.

Promotion opportunities at work, meanwhile, were not long in coming for me. My first opportunity came when I was still just 18, but I declined this offer as I felt I was just not experienced enough (for postman higher grade); I just could not see myself comfortably giving instructions to men who had been in the job for 40 years. Three years later, in 1979, I was offered promotion again, and this time I accepted. Consequently, I spent six months at what we called SEDO – the South Eastern District Office, which was head office for its namesake district, situated in Borough High Street near London Bridge.

But the harsh truth was that I badly missed my previous job, location and mates at Blackheath. I really did love that place and the men I worked with. There were only about 60 of us there – a real happy "family" – compared with around 4 to 500 at SEDO. Blackheath was a delightful "patch." It was just like a separate little village – a community – within London. It was full of interesting people, beautiful architecture and parkland. It was, if you like, a village-in-a-city-in-the-country. As soon as you stepped outside its boundaries, you were back in the hubbub of London.

So I only stuck the new job for those six months. The system was such that, in effect, your old job was held open for you to return to it if you wished after this period, but not beyond. So I exercised that option, even though it meant returning to the lower pay level. I resumed my role at Blackheath as a postman/driver until 1982, when I found myself returning to Cornwall once more - and another big new chapter in my life.

Before I did that, though, there was some more fun to be had, notably when Jethro and I played a prank – or tried to – on one of our colleagues. There was a young postman called Steve Twitchett who – untypically in those days – was scruffy in his appearance, complete with long, greasy hair. He was a cheeky little blighter and was regularly receiving written warnings over his appearance and behaviour.

One day he went into a cubicle in the toilets. Jethro told me he was in there and we quickly worked up a practical joke to play on him – not least as some kind of revenge for his recent mouthings-off about drivers. We found two large pans with handles and filled them up with water. It seemed as if they weighed a ton. We carried them into the toilets, trying not to giggle in the process, and somehow managed to heave them up to the top of the row of cubicles.

The intention was to tip their contents over young Mr Twitchett, but, because they were so heavy and unwieldy, we actually ended up tipping them the wrong side, into the wrong cubicle. Instead of Mr Twitchett being on the receiving end, the honour fell to an inspector by the nickname of Gum Boil (so called because, in our eyes, he looked like one). We heard his reaction – it understandably put the poor man in a vile mood – but we managed to scarper at a rate of knots, with the result that no-one ever discovered who had performed the wicked deed. And we certainly weren't going to tell anyone!

During my time based in Blackheath, I also had the pleasure of working on the TPOs – the travelling post offices, i.e. the overnight trains. I used to fill in for anyone sick or on holiday. I worked on the Penzance to Plymouth trains and this suited me, as it meant I got the chance for extra visits to my mum and dad in Cornwall. For this work, I got three pay packets – the standard one, another for "inconvenience" and a third in a registered envelope, "from the Queen," as a bonus and thus upholding an age-old tradition.

I could not work for the Royal Mail today. So much has changed; standards have fallen so low. The postmen and women of today do not have the respect for themselves, or anything else for that matter, that we did. For instance, the amount of mail that goes missing, instead of reaching me at my home, is nobody's business. Similarly, the way so much mail is just left dumped on my step is heartbreaking to see.

Ditto the state they walk around in. In my days with the service, we were inspected every day before hitting the streets. There was no room for even a speck of dust on our shoes. Young Mr Twitchett stood out a mile then; now he would be in his element, with no-one batting an eyelid at the sight of him. But all that – my time with the Royal Mail – was put behind me once and for all when I headed back to Cornwall in 1982.

CHAPTER TEN

BACK TO CORNWALL,
BUT WITH SOME NASTY
SURPRISES IN STORE

As much as I loved London, and Blackheath in particular, I had always yearned to return to Cornwall. By 1982, I had been on the transfer list for five years, but had never quite made it back to a postal district in the Duchy; no doubt, there was always somebody more genuinely local than me whenever such a vacancy came up.

So, to the considerable shock of my colleagues and superiors, I simply decided that I was going back to Cornwall anyway. I had spent many a happy weekend there and the pull was just too strong. I gave up my postal career in the confident belief – misplaced, as it turned out – that I would have no difficulty finding a job of some sort in Cornwall.

The reality was that jobs were scarce there. In March, 1982, I headed back west to live once more with my parents, who had moved by now to Carharrack. I soon discovered that things were changing fast and firms were closing down. Nonetheless, I was lucky, and before very long I was back in employment.

I was offered a job with Redruth-based Griggs, builders' merchants. The offer came from Paul Bowden. I had got to know Paul because he used to come in to the Clinton Club, in Redruth, for a drink. My future brother-in-law, Mike Gould, was head steward there, and he had a word with Paul on my behalf. I was taken on as a lorry driver, on a temporary basis. I had secured my HGV driver's licence while with the Post Office in London.

I became very good friends with Paul, who was yard manager with Griggs, and we had a fair bit in common, not least in the world of sport. I worked for most of that year with Griggs. I was taken on with a view to filling in for sickness and holiday leave, but in fact Paul saw to it that I was never short of work. I got on very well, too, with Mr Grigg, the owner of the business, and Brian May, who was a director and also a big Redruth rugby fan. There were seven of us employees – myself, Alan Burley, Gordon Richardson, Mike Bray, "Sabu" and the two Dereks, surnames not recalled.

Away from work, Paul was chairman of selectors for the Cornwall rugby team and a keen cricketer. He also used to cover rugby and cricket for the local newspapers. He had a lovely smile, a warm, kind glint in his eye, and was genuinely a much-loved guy.

Apart from the job with Griggs, one of my own main reasons for being grateful to him was his kindness in taking me with him when he needed to go out of the county to watch potential Cornwall "caps" playing for their club sides. It was fascinating to see the game from a different viewpoint – and meeting players and officials from the various county unions.

Whilst with Paul, I also drove members of the Cornwall rugby team around to various training locations in the old Clinton Club minibus, as part of the preparations for the county matches. This vehicle was a genuine old banger – and it was quite amazing that we managed to get it going at all.

Paul died in 2010, God rest his soul. I renewed my contact with him some years after my time with Griggs, when I had left Cornwall once more only to return yet again.

Given that my Griggs job, for all Paul's support, was only ever temporary, in 1983 I became aware of a vacancy for a lorry driver with Cornish Linen and successfully applied for it. Alas, this turned out to be not the best job I ever had, with my new employers applying some Draconian policies. For instance, the male employees were not allowed to speak to their female colleagues – yes, unbelievable – and if you weren't actually driving you were permitted a ten-minute tea break, which had to be completed on the dot. (My own view of the rule forbidding no talking to the ladies was "I don't think so," and I ended up courting one of them!)

I had been working for Griggs for three months when I woke up one morning feeling absolutely terrible. Initially, my mother was very angry as she suspected I was simply nursing a giant hangover from my previous night's drinking. But I didn't "do" hangovers – or at least I never drank heavily the night before I knew I would be working.

I never made it into work that day, nor for a long time afterwards. By mid-afternoon, I was going from bad to worse, and when she came home at around 5 pm even my mum could see instantly that I was really poorly. She called out the doctor, who said it was flu and prescribed Paracetamol. Two hours later, I was in an even worse state – with an unbelievably agonising headache. Mum got the doctor back and he took one look at me and called an ambulance to take me to hospital.

It turned out that I had meningitis, and I was in Truro Hospital for two weeks. Scary! I knew how deadly meningitis was, even though it transpired that mine was not the worst form. It was quite bad enough! Let me tell you how bad it was. I had to have a "lumber punch" injection into my spine. This is normally an acutely painful experience, the worst kind of injection you can possibly have. Yet I didn't feel a thing because I had so much pain and discomfort elsewhere; my head felt as though it was going to explode at any moment.

A month or two later, when I was well on the recovery road once more, my sporting life took a new turn when I was having a drink in the Coppice Inn in Lanner and was approached by the manager of the village football team. We already knew each other and he asked me if I would like to play for his team in the coming season, in the Cornwall Mining League Division One.

I readily agreed and took up my role once more as a flying winger! This was a nice little tonic for me after such an unsettling period on the health front. As I was still recovering, doctor's orders were that I could only do light training for a while, and I started this at the end of July. I had a good season with Lanner; they were good lads. I don't recall anything special for Yours Truly, though – no double hat-tricks or sendings-off!

The following close season, I was on the move again, this time agreeing to play for Pete Harvey in his Heathcotes team in Camborne, who were quite a powerful force on the Cornish soccer scene at the time, having risen from what was essentially a works/social team to one now competing in the

Cornwall Combination League, just one step away from the county's most senior league then.

Pete was a great character and I was very happy to sign for him. He also brought in a Cornish sporting legend, Salvotori Nucifero, who we always called Salvo. He was a welterweight boxer who only a few months previously had fought Colin Jones at the Royal Albert Hall for the British title, with Colin winning. (Colin, a Welshman, represented Great Britain at the 1976 Summer Olympics in Montreal, Canada.)

Salvo and I hit it off straightaway – and looking back, I'm not sure if this was a good thing or a bad thing. (Sorry, Salvo – only kidding!) He and I loved to chase the women. He was a real character and always had a glint in his eye and a warm smile.

As with Lanner, I had just the one season with Heathcotes. At the same time, I was playing a bit of rugby with Redruth Grammar School Old Boys, a team set up by my good mate Paul Bowden and captained by Mike Gould. So I was able to keep myself really fit – as often as not, if I had no soccer match one weekend, I could play rugby instead. There were even times when I would have a double-day of action, playing rugby in the morning and soccer in the afternoon!

I had got involved in the Old Boys rugby team after I had come back from a soccer match one Saturday afternoon and gone into the Clinton Club for a drink. The rugby team, or most of them, were already there and they were all pretty dejected because they had suffered a hammering. Their lack of success, it transpired, was partly due to their lack of a kicker – the guy who can reliably convert the tries and kick the penalties. I told them I could place a football on a sixpence, indicating that I could be just as good with a rugby ball (although I never had been a kicker in that game) and they took me up and got me into their team – although, strangely, I never was given the kicking duties. I played on the wing for them and made a number of appearances, on and off, for a couple of seasons.

Much "business" was conducted at the Clinton Club, and that is where I was suddenly consumed by the next Big Idea for my life, one that was to see me literally "hitting the road" again, and in somewhat bizarre fashion . . .

CHAPTER 11

MY GRAND PLAN – OFF INTO THE DARK, AND THE SNOW

It was a cold, grim winter's day, even by Cornwall's standards – a Friday afternoon in early February, 1985 – and I was sitting in the bar at the Clinton Club, chatting with my future brother-in-law, Mike Gould, and a few locals. Gradually, my company diminished, until I realised that I was actually on my own. The others were either playing pool or had left, and Mike was busy talking to another punter.

And that's when it hit me. "What am I going to do with my life?" I wondered. For the previous few months, I had been working as a labourer, starting off on the bottle line, at Redruth Brewery.

The Cornish Linen job had only been temporary, and I had been laid off there. It was a funny situation. As a temporary employee, you were taken on for 13 weeks at a time. At the end of each such period, you received two letters – one sacking you and another reinstating you! Or at least that was the hope, that you would receive both the letters rather than just the one saying bye-bye. Well, I got just the one shortly before Christmas. (Great timing.) I had earlier been told that I was likely to be made up to a permanent position there early in the New Year, but that was not to be.

I had no idea how long it would be, if ever, before they re-employed me, and in the meantime I was increasingly thinking that it was time to "move on" once more. So, with the big New Idea rapidly taking shape in my head, I left the Clinton and wandered over to the Oxford Inn to see if my mate Lindsey Mayne was there so that I could tell him that I was going to head back to London!

I had already said farewell to another old school mate, Brian ("Mona") Hull, not that he realised it. As I was leaving the Clinton, I looked around, saw him there and said "Bye, Bri." We had sat next to each other at school and we still see each other today, but I didn't let on the special significance of that "bye" in the Clinton.

Lindsey Mayne wasn't in the Oxford, so I sat down there on my own, and it didn't take me long to put a lot of flesh onto the bones of my idea – my grand plan. I drank my beer and then rushed home – to start packing. Not a suitcase, just my large sports holdall. I just put in some bare essentials and precious little else.

At about 6 pm, I set off again, with that holdall, and in freshly falling snow. I didn't say what I was doing or where I was going. Mum wasn't at home and Dad just sat there, looking stunned. I said: "Goodbye, Dad," and was off. I just wanted to get on with it before giving anyone the chance to persuade me to change my mind.

The snow had in fact been falling for quite a while and so there was a fairly thick layer of it on the ground. I trudged through it, in pitch black darkness, in the direction of the old A30, with a view to hitch-hiking to The Smoke. This – from home to the A30 – was a distance of about a mile. Home was now Roseland Gardens in Redruth, with Mum and Dad having moved there from Carharrack (and living next door to my future wife, Gail).

Because of the conditions – the white world – I did not immediately see any traffic; there was nothing coming into or out of Redruth. So I made it to the A30 – and still no traffic in sight – and carried on walking eastwards. I got as far as Fraddon – fully 15 miles away – having (yes, I admit it) clearly taken total leave of my senses. It was about 10 pm by now. I stood at the junction that used to split there, looked back, and saw in the distance what appeared to be a single-decker bus coming towards me.

I thought: "At last, I'll get a bus that should take me a good stretch of the way." Not surprisingly, I felt frozen stiff by now. I was wearing a lumberjack-type coat, but it was not waterproof – and the snow was still falling. I waved to the driver of the "bus" and it turned out that it was a coach, and empty of passengers. The driver stopped and asked me what on earth I was doing. I said I needed to get to London, and he replied that he could take me as far as Plymouth.

I was really grateful for that ride – and the warmth inside the coach! He asked me what I was planning on doing once I had got to London, and I explained that I was going to be like him, a long distance coach driver – all part of my grand plan!

In those days, there was a sort of TV "Jobcentre" service with vacancies displayed on Ceefax, and I had seen that London Transport were advertising for drivers for buses in London. I had earlier applied, twice, for just such a job and had been turned down on both occasions. I assumed they had thought that, as a country bumpkin living in Cornwall, I would be unsuited for the London streets.

For quite some time, I had got it into my head that I wanted to be a long distance coach driver. I loved working with people, and you're very much on your own when you're driving a lorry all over the place. To be a coach driver, I needed to get my PSV (public service vehicle) driver's licence. So my thinking was that if I could get taken on by London Transport I could get my PSV licence and stay with them for a year or two before progressing to coach-driving.

I explained all this to that night-time coach driver who took me, ever so slowly and carefully, to Plymouth in the snow. He dropped me off at a roundabout in that city, by which time it was around midnight. I was cold and hungry, but I was not to be deflected or deterred – I had a plan and I was clinging to it! And I certainly wasn't panicking – I've never been that type.

After about ten minutes, a car pulled up in response to my hitch-hiker signal and I said "anywhere along the main London road" would do. The driver was heading for a village somewhere near Exeter and so I got in, feeling pleased with myself once more. Alas, he turned out to be a weirdo. As we got closer to Exeter, he asked if I would like to go back to his place for the night, adding that his wife "wouldn't mind." I told him to stop the car. I grabbed my holdall and got the hell out of it! I didn't know where I was . . . and began walking again, in the snow. It was still pitch black, too, of course, and I soon began to "freeze" once more. All I knew was that I must be heading in the general direction of Exeter Services. I got there around three quarters of an hour later. By now it must have been well past one in the morning.

In amongst all the parked lorries, I looked around for one that might be going to London – and preferably one of Cornish origin. I duly found one with "Penzance" on its side and so I stood there, beside the cab, awaiting the return of the driver. Fortune smiled on me, because it turned out I actually knew the driver. When he came into view, I recognised him as a guy who used to work at Redruth Brewery, collecting the used barrels, at the same time as I was there.

He confirmed that he was London-bound and said he would drop me off somewhere in the East End. On the way up, we stopped at a service station in Gloucestershire and he offered to pay for my breakfast, which was fantastic as I didn't have a lot of money on me and didn't know what my immediate future held in store for me.

Alas, we had just sat down to our hearty-looking breakfast, at around 4 am – hadn't even taken our first mouthful – when there was suddenly the most almighty commotion as the doors burst open and in swept the police, telling us all to evacuate the building immediately because there was a suspected bomb on the premises! "Just my bloody luck," I thought. I had survived the freezing snow only to be hit by a bomb scare. I even asked one of the policemen if I could take my breakfast with me, but he said: "No, get out now." I had eaten nothing since a Cornish pasty in the Clinton Club the previous afternoon.

So we resumed our journey – we figured there was no point in hanging around waiting, as it was likely to be ages before the all-clear was given – and I was dropped off in London's East End around 6 am. I didn't really know the East End very well (as opposed to South East London, which I knew like the back of my hand), and so I figured that my next step should be to head for the West End, get something to eat at long last, and find somewhere to stay. The weather by now had changed. It was still cold but dry, with no snow in London yet.

Precise details of what followed are a bit vague now, but I remember going to some sort of charity place and asking where I could find somewhere to stay until I got myself properly sorted. They directed me to another place, which turned out to be full, and they in turn re-directed me to somewhere else in the West End. This, I recall, was quite a famous place for the homeless, although its name escapes me. The people here made a phone call to a place in Willesden, North West London, and established that there was a vacancy there for me, and that they would look after me. I got a bed there and stayed there for several weeks. So my next hurdle was the quest for employment

Linda and Mum with Clare on her second birthday, 1991

Clare, James and Carrie-Anne, 1993

"My gang!" Left to right: James, Andrew,
Clare, Carrie-Anne and Matthew

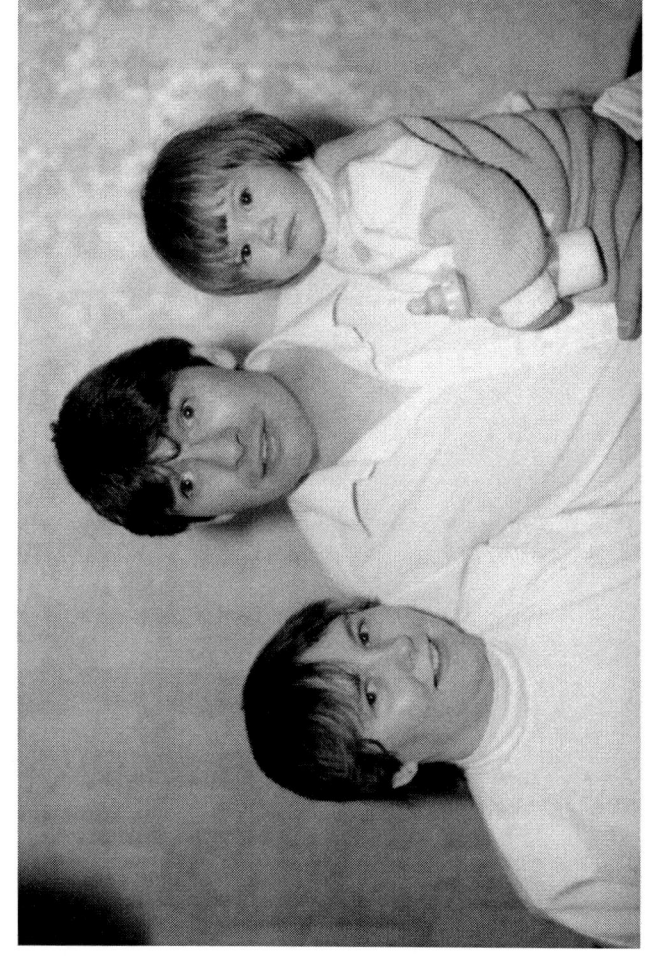

Linda, Clare and me, 1990

Best friends – James and Matthew

Two more "best friends" – Clare and Carrie-Anne

(Bath) Team Maloney, left to right: Andrew, James, Matthew, Clare, Carrie-Anne

Have truck will travel. My constant companion for the
England 1990 World Cup Finals in Italy.

The beer which Peter Beardsley gave to me, and which we had to leave behind in Bologna.

No room left on the truck. Gutted – haha!

Me with New Order's gold disc in Bologna.

"Mere boys then!" A young me with an equally fresh-looking
David Platt, after a training session in Asti.

CHAPTER 12

MORE JOB CHANGES . . .
AND OUR FIRST HOME
OF OUR OWN

From my temporary Willesden base, I applied for a job on the buses, through the Baker Street base of London Transport. They asked me where I was staying – well, at least I had an address – and they told me they were holding interviews at the Wembley Jobcentre one afternoon at 2 pm. I should be there, if I was interested, and they gave me a document to present on arrival.

I was interviewed by an inspector and took a maths test, and then had to wait a couple of weeks before I received a letter, still at the Willesden hostel. The letter advised me to go to Chiswick for a preliminary sight examination and driving test. I did so, passed the sight test and was then sent out on a London Routemaster double-decker bus, just with an inspector. He sat in the seat immediately behind the driver's cab and explained where he wanted me to go.

He expressly told me how he would like me to drive if I had passengers on board the bus, in the London traffic. I had driven lorries and knew London fairly well. We duly headed out of Chiswick bus station and made towards the West End. I did everything right – or so I thought. After returning to the bus station, I had to wait in an auditorium, with a lot of other people, until my name was called.

Each one called ahead of me went off to a separate room, but when the inspector who had accompanied me on the bus came out and called my name, he went berserk, tearing me off a strip in front of everybody else. I thought "What's he on about?" Truth to tell, he put me into a state of shock. Apparently, I had done just one thing wrong – when I had initially left the station, I had not stopped at the bus sign at the exit. I had treated it as a Give Way sign and had gone straight out into the road.

This was so embarrassing; I felt such a fool. But, as he later explained, he did this, in front of everyone else, precisely in order that I would never forget it, and never do such a thing again. Clever, really. And I had passed the test! I was told to report to Harlesden bus station at 8 am the following Monday. This was only just round the corner from where I was staying.

I reported for work half an hour early, at 7.30 am, the expectation being that I would now be trained up to PSV licence standard, so that I could drive buses WITH passengers in. I enthusiastically produced my reference papers – only to be told by the lady behind a desk that I would not be able to do anything that day because there was an inspectors' strike on! Wonderful, I thought; here we go again. I asked how long the strike was expected to last and the lady replied: "How long is a piece of string?" It was all news to me; I hadn't even read anything about the bally strike. The lady said they would be in touch with me again as soon as the strike was over, so that I could resume my training.

But in the meantime I must have cut a sorry figure as I trudged out of that bus station again, thoroughly fed up with life. The pressing fact was that I needed a job sooner rather than later. I was walking along Harlesden High Street when the local Jobcentre display window came into view – I had never seen one so big – and I noticed that there were two or three advertisements for lorry driver vacancies.

So I went in and enquired about one of them, which looked quite good to me. I thought: "If I get this, it will do me until the bus inspectors' strike is over." They took my details and gave me a number to phone. I spoke to a Mr Fred Joyce, who asked me to come over for interview at Alfro-Anglex, importers and exporters of china and glass, based in Smithfield.

Fred, the company's transport manager, interviewed me and told me he had a few more candidates to see, so he wanted me to phone in the next day. The outcome of that call was a summons back to Fred's office straightaway, whereupon I was offered the job and asked to start work the following Monday (it was now a Thursday or Friday).

I was to be driving all over the country, delivering the glass and china to various company outlets and exhibitions. It immediately struck me as a very friendly company. I liked everyone and got on well with Fred, who was a proper Cockney from the East End.

Once I learnt that the bus inspectors' strike was over, I concluded that I liked my new job so much that I would prefer to stay in it anyway. London Transport contacted me, but I explained my new circumstances and they accepted my decision in good spirit. I stayed with Alfro-Anglex for four years and Fred and I became good friends. He commuted from his home in Farnborough, Hampshire – where I would go and stay for the occasional weekend away.

I had long since moved out of the Willesden hostel and into a flat in Greenwich. I had also started courting my first wife, Linda, whom I had met in Cornwall. I was still going back to Cornwall quite a lot, staying with Mum and Dad. I had met Linda on the Thursday before Easter, in the Red Lion pub in Redruth; she was 21 and I was 29.

Linda was working in a nursing home in Green Lane, Redruth, and so it was something of a long distance courtship, but eventually she moved up to London and got a job as a nurse at Lewisham Hospital. We were married in March, 1988, at Ayr in Scotland, as Linda's mother came from Ayr and I also had strong family connections with the area, of course. A year later, on May 24, 1989, while we were still living in our flat in Greenwich, Linda gave birth to our first child, daughter Clare. Great pride all round! In fact, I think you could safely say that at that particular moment I was the proudest dad in the whole world

Clare was born at 9 pm in Greenwich Hospital at the end of a glorious early summer's day. I attended the birth, which was straightforward, and my mum and dad had come up from Cornwall to join us. Clare came into the world weighing 6lbs 2ozs. She was a little gem – and she still is!

That year, 1989, proved to be a red letter year for us in more ways than one. In August, I was offered a "new job" by the company I was now working for, Greenwich-based European and General Shipping, whom I had joined in the previous year. They were opening up a state of the art brand new office and warehouse complex at Speke in Liverpool – close to Liverpool Airport and on the site of the former Dunlop tyre plant – and invited me to relocate with them. The directors, Mike and Alan Dee, spelt it all out for me, and believe me, I could have snapped their hands off; I needed no persuading. It was a great opportunity to get my family out of London.

The firm gave me time to house-hunt and we eventually bought a three-bedroom semi-detached property in Runcorn, a new town just 20 miles from Liverpool. This was the first home of our own. It was in Helston Close (now there was a reminder of Cornwall!) and close to the M56 and the link to the M6. I had just turned 31; I was in a job that I greatly enjoyed and now I was going to live in a well nigh perfect location for it.

I felt I already knew Runcorn quite well, as it happened, because I had had a lot of dealings with that town in my job, driving the lorry up there two or three times a week and getting to know quite a few people – genuine friends - in the town. Through one of these friends, I also managed to get a job for Linda in Halton, which is also part of Runcorn. Runcorn is a most unusual place in that it is one of the very few places that can claim to have been built on two canals and a river – the Manchester Ship Canal, the Bridgewater Canal and the River Mersey.

We quickly settled in our new home, which was just 200 yards from our local pub, the Halton Arms. It was in there that I met one of my first new mates up north, none other than boxer Robin Reid. Robin was still on the way up at that stage. His greatest successes came when he won the light middleweight bronze medal for Great Britain at the 1992 Summer Olympics in Barcelona, Spain, and then the WBC (World Boxing Council) super middleweight title four years later. Robin added acting to his career a few years later. In 2010, he took over a lead role in the controversial film "Killer Bitch" from cage fighter Alex Reid, who had walked out of the film. When I first met him, he would have been 18. He trained in a gym next door to the pub and would come in for a pint twice a week. We played darts and pool together and talked about his ambitions. I followed his progress with great interest.

CHAPTER 13

BAD TIMES WITH BURGLARIES . . . BUT MY WILDEST DREAMS COME TRUE

$\mathbf{W}$e were made to feel very welcome in our new home and territory – with just the one big exception, or rather two. We had the horrible double-whammy experience of twice being burgled, first in November of that year, just three months after moving into our new home, and then again in the summer of 1991.

The first time, the three of us, myself, Linda and Clare, were away for a long weekend to take in a wedding at Ayr. As soon as we got back and I walked in through the front door, I could tell something was wrong; the house just felt so cold – ice-cold. It turned out that our uninvited guests had broken in through our patio doors at the rear of the house, and because they had not been closed again properly the air was getting in and keeping the temperature well down.

The scumbags took just about everything we had that was of any value to us. Virtually all our possessions were brand new, as the proverbial newly-wed couple in their "new" home. These included my wedding ring, which I never got back. The stolen items also included my driving licence, which the police found – altered – in Chester.

I had left the ring behind when we went to Scotland for the wedding; I often took it off because otherwise it tended to get in the way when I was lifting and tugging things in my job. This time, unfortunately, I had completely forgotten to put it back on before we set off. The burglars also helped themselves to our microwave oven, our TV and video recorder plus a host of other wedding presents. They went through all Linda's drawers and basically cleaned us out. They had had the whole weekend to do it and it was a horrible discovery for us when we got back.

Our house backed on to open fields and so there's no denying that we were vulnerable. With our neighbour being away at the same time as well, it had been even easier for the burglars, who just had to climb over the fence and then cross our garden and break in through those patio doors. This was the one and only time we ever claimed on our insurance – we had to, as we were talking losses running into several thousands of pounds. It was devastating, sickening; a lovely weekend for us all had been utterly ruined. Needless to say, those patio doors, which were on the old side, were replaced with much more secure new ones.

Linda and I were both strong personalities, and for all that we had been deeply hurt we quickly decided that there was only one thing for it and that was to get on with our lives. So we got all the insurance and so on sorted – and moved on.

Our second burglary was more of a dramatic event and occurred with us all still in the house. It was still dark, just, and must have been shortly after 4 a.m. when Linda woke up with a start and told me she had heard a noise from downstairs. I shot out of bed and rushed downstairs – stark naked – to find two young men scarpering down the garden and frantically climbing over the fence. All they had managed to take was Linda's expensive watch and as they ran across the lawn they each dropped a screw driver.

Linda later told me that the previous evening she had left a narrow kitchen window open, to let air in overnight. This window was so narrow, in fact, that you could scarcely imagine a cat, let alone a human being, squeezing through it. But one of them had managed to do just that and let the other in through the door, unlocking it from the inside.

Again, it was an appalling experience to know that people had broken into our home, but again we did not let it get us down any more than absolutely necessary. For my part, I was so determined to catch the little pieces of pond life that for several weeks afterwards I routinely got up around 3 a.m. every night and wandered around our nearby streets in the hope that I might spot them trying to repeat the feat at another property.

The nearest I got to a successful outcome was seeing a couple of young men who did look quite similar to those I could recall in our own garden, but I couldn't be sure and, more to the point, I couldn't really approach them anyway unless they were actually trying to break in somewhere, which they weren't. Linda didn't mind me performing this vigilante role. In effect, she just shrugged her shoulders and let me get on with it; she knew what I was like! I eventually gave this up after about four weeks.

For all our stoicism, it took a while for things to get back to normal. I'm talking months, in fact. Every time we heard a sound, we would immediately think that the buggers were back. We would be wide awake in a split second. As they say, you lose more than just your physical possessions when you've been burgled. Nonetheless, that is all very much in the past now. Touch wood, that was the last time we were ever burgled, and such thoughts are no longer at the forefront of our minds.

In between those two ghastly burglary events, there had been further memorable highlights and big changes in my life. In December, 1989, we prepared for Clare's first Christmas. We were joined by my Mum and Dad and sister Caroline and it must have been one of my happiest Christmases ever. Clare may have been only seven months old, but she was still old enough to have some inkling of what was going on and to appreciate her host of presents. Buying Christmas presents for your first child, and watching her try to unwrap them, is a magical experience you simply never forget. It was our first Christmas as a new family. My mother's face lit up, loving the thrill of her first grandchild opening her presents on this very special day.

In the meantime, we were just days away from a train of events that would lead to the most memorable and enjoyable phase of my whole working life. I had been heavily involved in preparations – transporting of staff and equipment for outside broadcasting - for the BBC's coverage of the Commonwealth Games in Auckland, New Zealand, in January-February 1990.

European and General Shipping had the logistical contract for the Olympian Association. I had brought all the sports equipment back from Heathrow when it came back from Seoul in 1988, so now we were going to take all the sports equipment and luggage, as well as the outside radio broadcasting equipment, to Auckland.

I had been very busy on this during the run-up to Christmas, and then on Boxing Day I had to travel down to London to oversee the final part of the operation prior to the BBC team's flight out. It should all have been a very simple affair; instead, it turned out to be more of a nightmare.

On arrival in London, I told them that all the boxes and crates in which everything was to be packed had to be specially treated first, to guard against bugs and so on. Any crates bound for the likes of New Zealand and Australia had to be sprayed with anti-fungal chemicals. It transpired that everything had been loaded up – but without the crucial treatment being applied first.

It was the day after Boxing Day now, which meant that just about everyone who was qualified to do the work and who would normally be expected to respond quickly to any such emergency call for help was still either on holiday, unavailable or severely unwilling to return to work. Luckily, I knew a guy who lived near Chatham in Kent who could do this treatment job and I managed to get hold of him and persuade him to come to our rescue.

There were over a hundred crates involved, of various sizes, and these were loaded up on to my ten-ton lorry for me to drive them down from the BBC Television Centre in Woodlane to Chatham (for returning to the BBC once the work had been done).

Far from being a day I wanted to forget, however, this turned out to be the one when all my wildest dreams started to come true. I knew I would have a lot of time to kill while I waited for the treatment work to be done, so I adjourned to the Castle pub in North Acton, which was opposite a sizable BBC base across the road. I knew a lot of BBC folk and they in turn would know where to find me in an emergency (mobile phones were not a part of everyday life then, of course).

I remember there were two delightful log fires roaring away in that pub; it all looked very welcoming and festive, and I was dying for a pint. I had just got my poison when I suddenly heard a familiar voice, in a heavy Scottish accent, enquire: "What are you doin' here?" I turned round to see my old mate Ian "Krankie" Tough, of the "The Krankies" 1980s and 90s TV fame. The Krankies were Ian and his wife Janette, a comedy duo who portrayed a schoolboy and his father among other characters. They also released their own music single.

I had known Ian and Janette for some two or three years and we duly shook hands and exchanged festive greetings. The pub had been the link for us. I asked where Janette was and he said she wouldn't be long. He added, with a wink: "When she does arrive, I've only just got here, right?" "Okay, no problems," I agreed. We chatted for about half an hour and then Janette joined us, along with a couple of her own friends.

"Hello, James, Merry Christmas," she said, followed immediately by: "How long has he (Ian) been here?" I couldn't resist replying: "Oh, about two hours!" Ian's face sank – it was a picture. Janette, who was very much on the short side, cheerfully punched him on the arm. They were true comedians and rarely stopped laughing. Back at the bar, and with both of us sporting grins as wide as the Clyde, Ian promised me: "I will get you for that." And he did! Much sooner than he had expected.

We continued to chat away, the fires carried on roaring and the pub got more and more crowded . . . and then the numbers swelled still further with the arrival of three imposing looking gentlemen. One of them was very tall – around seven feet, seriously - and I heard him ask the landlord if James Maloney was in. Ian and I looked at each other and I thought: "Shit, who the hell are they?" Ian must have sensed my fear and – seizing his opportunity for "revenge" – shouted across to them: "Hey Mister, this is James Maloney over here."

The giant, with his colleagues, came over and offered me his outstretched hand. "Merry Christmas, James," he said. "My name's Adrian Titcombe, from the FA, and this is David Bloomfield (son of radio commentator and former Arsenal, West Ham United and Birmingham City player Jimmy Bloomfield). David was travel manager and the third gentleman in the party, Les Walker, was introduced as the FA's head of security.

Well, we straightaway got on like a house on fire. With Ian still right up beside me, ear-wigging, I politely asked how I could help these gentlemen. Adrian explained that they had heard about the work I had been doing for the Olympic Association and how I had fitted in so well with the team albeit with the knack of remaining largely in the background.

"That's because I'm shy by nature," I said. But Adrian countered: "That's exactly what we're looking for. Would you like to come and work with the England football team?" I just about managed to remain standing. I was stunned, gobsmacked, you name it. Ian broke the silence, and the ice, by advising me: "You'd be better off working for the Scotland team; you won't be away from your family for so long!" Cue laughter all round.

When we had all re-composed ourselves, I looked at the big man and said: "Yes, please." Adrian said: "We'll be in touch." We shook hands again; he wished us a Happy New Year and the trio left us in peace once more. I asked Ian: "Did I just dream that?" "Not at all," he confirmed. We told Janette what had just happened . . . and the whisky flowed.

CHAPTER 14

MY LONG AND WINDING ROAD TO 'THE PARADISE ISLE'

I arrived back in Runcorn on December 30, 1989, a day late and still a bit hung over, to find that Mum, Dad and sister Caroline had already returned to Cornwall – and I was still in Dreamland! I was struggling to believe that this was happening to me. Normally, I could not win a two-horse race – and yet now I had landed a plum job with the England football team, and I was Italy-bound for the 1990 World Cup Finals. It just didn't come any better than this.

For a short while, I actually did begin to wonder whether it was all too good to be true – because the weeks went by without me hearing anything more. I eagerly read up everything I could lay my hands on regarding the England team and the venues for their World Cup matches, with the first one in Sardinia against Jack Charlton's Ireland on June 11. And what a coincidence this was, bearing in mind my memories of him at school (and of my mum reading the riot act to him!) I came to regard Sardinia as "the paradise isle" – because that is precisely what it was in my eyes – but there was a long and winding road, in more ways than one, before I finally got there.

One afternoon in March, I had a phone call from Alan Dee, the managing director of my employers, European and General Shipping, who ran the company with his brother Mike. Alan told me to be in the head office in Greenwich for an 11 am meeting the next day. On arrival, I met up with the Dees and Adrian Titcombe, one of those three FA gentlemen who had headhunted me in the pub and who I now knew to be the FA's head of competitions, rules and regulations.

Now – I knew – it was all starting. I'm not ashamed to admit that I was incredibly excited at this time. I sat there for fully two hours listening very intently to these people outlining exactly what was expected of me in my new role. Countless elaborate plans and arrangements were being drawn up – with me at the heart of it all! It was truly fascinating. Not once did any of these people say, or intimate: "Mess up and you're out." They didn't need to; they knew I would not mess up!

It was made clear to me that I would be looking after the players in the form of all their needs and wants – luggage, food, playing kits, training kit, medical equipment, computers, golf clubs and so on and so on - and it was the first time in the history of the FA that they had appointed someone to this specific position. Crumbs – now I was making history as well as anticipating the time of my life! That was about right, I thought. It could only happen to me – right place, right time! We were talking about a party of some 50 people – the playing squad of 22 plus (dare I say it!) various "hangers-on."

This meeting was never an interview – just a briefing session. It was as clear as day to me now, even if it hadn't been before, that I had effectively been headhunted for this job. My heart was bursting with pride. (And it still is, come to that!)

The next two months dragged somewhat, except for one day when I had to take 26 sets of Wilson golf clubs to Bisham Abbey Golf Club, where I would meet the England players for the first time. That was a good day, although a lasting memory is just how snooty the club and some of its members were.

As I was watching the players knocking their golf balls about, a member came up close to me and pointedly counted them, followed by the remark, delivered in a crusty upper-class accent: "Four or five – yes, that's about the right number." It dawned on me what he was doing – he was assessing the proportion of black players in the England squad. How would he react nowadays, I wonder?

In the club itself, you could tell by the members' body language that they had mixed feelings about this "invasion" of their hallowed territory. The unspoken message – at least so far as I read it – was: "We're glad of the showpiece opportunity to be able to say that we have been chosen by a national sports team . . . . but we're not really entirely comfortable with your sort here; we'll tolerate it, but it's as well that it's not for long." Well, that's what I very easily imagined these types saying, anyway.

It was a strange feeling meeting so many international footballers, for the first time. I didn't know who to approach first, so I got a set of clubs off the truck and handed the first set to Bryan Robson. I asked him if he could get the rest of the players to come on over for their sets of clubs. He obliged, they came over, and I handed them out. They were very polite; some were very good golfers and some had never previously held a club! Steve McMahon was one of the former and he went on to win the little-known World Cup Golf Competition in Italy. I spent a lovely afternoon watching the lads knock the balls about. This is living all right, I thought, and I was really looking forward to the World Cup now.

On the morning of Saturday, May 19, I was London-bound once more and well and truly on my way to Italy after kissing Linda and Clare (now almost one year old) goodbye. I would be staying overnight with my friends Norman and Julie White in Greenwich prior to boarding the Dover-Calais ferry the next day. Norman was a huge scouser, built like a brick toilet house, and worked as a glass fitter. Julie was a buyer for Top Shop. She was fashion-mad and a great-looking woman with a lovely personality.

On arrival in London, I first went for my final briefing session at my employers' head office in Greenwich. This session was chiefly concerned with sorting out all the shipping documents. This fundamentally involved a "carnet" – a document allowing the importation of certain goods to countries without paying customs duty. This was basically covering all the stuff that everyone in the FA party would be taking out of the country and bringing back in, and some of its requirements struck me as pretty stupid, but we'll let that pass!

Then it was on to the Royal George pub to meet up with Norman and Julie and various others. These included "Pissey Chrissey", so named for obvious reasons, real name Chris French, who was always to be found at the bar. He was a lovely fellow – a former mate of mine from my Post Office days who absolutely loved his beer. Sadly, bearing in mind just how much of his beloved beer he must have consumed down the years, I very much doubt if he is still with us now.

It seemed everyone in the pub was delighted for me and telling me "well done" and wishing me all the best. These people included some of the hardest criminals around, I might add, who had even been made the subject of a TV crime documentary.

On the Sunday, May 20, I was joined by the guy who was to be my travelling companion all the way to Sardinia – Gordon Bridges, also from European and General Shipping. He was going to be setting up the computers for the Metropolitan Police. England soccer fans had a very bad reputation at that time and Gordon was basically going out to Italy ahead of the big event to work with that country's own police force in identifying known British thugs and preventing them from attending the matches if they turned up for them. These hooligans would be turned back at the border.

Gordon and I were travelling in an Iveco truck which, as it turned out, was now seriously overweight. The combined tonnage of the vehicle and its cargo came to 7.5, which was four tons over the limit. Fortunately, we never got stopped, or at least not in respect of the weight. I reckon the value of our cargo must have come to something like £30,000 – at the very least. Perhaps we should have had an armed escort! Instead, it was just me and Gordon in the vehicle cabin, "guarding" all this gear for the Italy-bound England World Cup squad. That was quite a responsibility!

Anyway, we were now Genoa-bound and boarding the Dover-Calais ferry on the Sunday, to sail at 5 pm. I showed my carnet to the customs at Dover and – understandably but in very friendly fashion – they were intrigued by the nature of my cargo! We got the truck safely on board, checked in to our cabin and then made for the restaurant for a well-earned meal followed by a couple of hours' sleep – which was very surprising, given my state of excitement.

We arrived at Calais at around 10 pm and the French customs were great. Then it was the great overland trip, starting with a drive through the early hours on our way to Mont Blanc ("white mountain"), which holds the triple distinction of being the highest mountain in the Alps, Western Europe and the European Union. I was used to being on my own for my truck trips, so it was a treat to have Gordon with me and we got on well. He was a likable fellow.

At around 8 am the next day, we came across a transport café, so we pulled over and I retrieved my toiletries and towel and headed off for a shower and a shave. Only problem was, there was no shower! I was met by just a tiny sink – plus one old lady sitting there, taking money and "supervising" me! So I maintained my dignity by stripping off down to my underpants and having a sink wash. It still felt good – I was fresh at last! Gordon followed suit and we both had a good laugh over it.

And so it was time for Mont Blanc. I have known drivers to be stuck there for a week or more – victims of the dreaded Mont Blanc customs who are notorious for keeping you waiting and being just plain ****** awkward. First, you have to find a parking space. Then you go over to the officers, who can drive you mad with frustration. They then send you all of 50 yards over to the Italians – who are as different as chalk from cheese and make you warmly welcome! Anyway, after about three hours – not bad by these standards – we finally got the all-clear to carry on driving.

Feeling pleased with ourselves at this point, the mood lightened further as I was walking to the exit of Italian customs and Gordon, for some unknown reason, opened a door and walked straight into a broom cupboard! It was a real Mr Bean moment if ever there was one – Mr Bean at his best – and the tears streamed down my face with laughing. I'm pleased to report that Gordon eventually managed to locate the correct exit door okay.

Climbing up the mountain was slow going, to put it mildly. We must have been going at all of ten miles per hour, although in fairness we were stuck behind a much bigger lorry – a 40-tonner - and so would otherwise have gone a wee bit faster, no doubt. The vista to our side must have been awesome – except that we could see next to nothing because it was dark by now.

There was snow on the road and in places it was quite deep. We were driving on snow all the way up (we must ultimately have reached a height of some 5,000 feet above sea level), but I was a very experienced driver in such conditions and so I felt this was no problem. This road was in constant use, with the snow consequently well crushed – although it was still very slippery in places, plus that much more hazardous in the dark, of course.

Then came the Mont Blanc tunnel – all 13 kilometres of it – and this had its hairy moments, too. The lanes are very narrow, although nowadays they are much better lit following a serious fire in the tunnel in 1999. (In March of that year, 39 people died when a Belgian transport truck carrying flour and margarine caught fire in the tunnel. There had been 16 other truck fires in the tunnel over the previous 35 years.)

On the other side of the mountain, having emerged from the tunnel and heading downhill once more . . . it was pretty hellish at times! On occasions I literally had to stand on the brakes. It was ever so steep and one slip and we would have been over the precipice – there were no barriers. One mistake from me and we would have been goners. Gordon never spoke at this time, which was probably a very wise policy, and his face at the end of it all was ashen; maybe mine had known brighter moments, too! I had needed every last drop of my strength and concentration.

As dawn broke, the emerging view was awesome. We were still coming down the mountain and we began to see the Alps in all their glory, with little villages in the distance. This was Heaven (after the hell of the night!). Things must have been looking up because Gordon was even starting to get some of his colour back! His first words to me were: "You were great; well done." "Cheers for that, Gordie," I replied.

We arrived in Genoa mid-afternoon on the Tuesday, May 21. I parked at the ferry terminal and left Gordon to sort out documentation details while I went for a shower, a beer and a pizza. When I returned, I found Gordon in a state of mild panic in the waiting lounge. "There's no room for us on the ferry tonight," he said. "Leave it to me," I replied. During my final briefing meeting back in Greenwich, Adrian Titcombe had given me certain telephone numbers for use in just such a situation. These numbers were for top people in the Italian FA and various other departments. If I was in a fix, I was to ring one of these numbers and everything would be sorted out pronto.

It worked. Within 15 minutes of the phone call I made now, we had our boarding pass. The ship – taking us over to the Sardinian port of Porto-Torres - was scheduled to sail at 7 pm. We still had some three hours to kill, so I went to see the vessel's head loader. I explained to him who I was and what we were about, and that we needed to be first off the ship at the end of the trip.

But he said "no first." I countered "yes first." I went back to the truck and got some "goodies" – trinkets and other World Cup memorabilia – and returned with these for him as a gift. "For me?" he asked. "Yes," I confirmed, "now put my truck on your ship." "You sure?" he asked. "Yes, I'm sure," I insisted. (If only I hadn't.) He shook his head (pityingly, as it turned out), looked at me and said: "Okay, my friend."

In its own way, getting my truck onto that ship and its parking bay down below was worse than negotiating Mont Blanc in the snow at dead of night. Down below, of course, it was very dark, and it was a right old obstacle course for me with unclosed hatches all over the place. I carefully drove around them all and eventually parked my truck in the bows of the ship. Mission accomplished. Or so I thought.

For the moment, though, peace reigned once more and Gordon and I went to our respective cabins. Each cabin had four beds, so Gordon came into mine because we thought there was going to be plenty of room. But then a Sardinian woman and her two teenage daughters turned up, explaining that they, too, had booked into "my" cabin. So Gordon returned to his, and I sat there on my bunk thinking: "I'm in a cabin here with a woman and her two daughters, and none of them can speak any English. Great."

Then I heard a commotion outside the door. It gradually dawned on me what was happening. There was a man outside who was the woman's husband and, not unnaturally, he wanted to be in the same cabin as her. The upshot was that I surrendered "my" cabin and transferred next door with Gordon. This went down really well with the Sardinian family, especially the man, who took us to the bar and bought us a drink. They also kept an eye on all my stuff back in their cabin.

It was a 12-hour crossing on the ferry, so Gordon and I had a meal and a few beers and then got our heads down. We got up again at 5 am the next day and headed back to the restaurant for a coffee. I ordered an espresso, thinking it would be ordinary coffee, but I certainly got that one wrong! It was like liquid tar and came in just a very small cup – the size of a sherry glass. At least it was full of caffeine, which was handy for getting me going again. Once fully awake, I had a wash and shave before returning to the restaurant for breakfast.

Then it was time to go out on deck and watch the ship pulling into Porto-Torres. It was a beautiful, glorious summer morning and our first sighting of this "paradise isle" – the rich man's playground - certainly made a very big and lasting impression.

Once the berthing had been completed, with the ship all tied up alongside, Gordon and I headed down below, all set to drive our truck straight off and onto the road. Haha – no such luck! To my horror, we discovered that this ship, being rather old and limited in its facilities and functions, was NOT a ro-ro vessel. The vehicles using it did NOT roll on at one end and then roll off at the other. We were not going to be first off – we would be the very LAST! No wonder the head loader had been shaking his head back in Genoa; no wonder he had been so reluctant to say yes to my request, bribes and all, to take the truck right to the bow. If he had had better English, he could have explained to me that I was being anything but clever!

Two hours later, we were still on the ship – we were the last to leave! And once again I had to negotiate the obstacle course, in the dark, as I drove around the hatches and over metal ramps and ropes, on our way back to the stern once more. If anything, it was even more taxing this time, of course, because I had to do it all in reverse – but I'm pleased to say that I once again managed it all without any scrapes.

It was very difficult and slow-going, and the sweat was pouring off me. So much for the benefits of my earlier shower! Anyway, we finally made it, left our ferry behind us, and drove off for Cagliari, the main town in the south of the island.

CHAPTER 15

I ENTER THE LAP OF LUXURY
ON PARADISE ISLE
... AND THE TOURNAMENT
STARTS FOR REAL

The drive south, the hundred miles or so of it, was actually uneventful, would you believe! We saw lots of people on the way – and lots of horse-drawn carts – and the roads were much the same standard as ours in the UK, with no shortage of potholes! Our destination was the five-star beach-side Hotel Is Morus in the small town of Pula. We were the first to arrive, ahead of the main England World Cup squad, officials and hangers on. This would be the first of several England camps for the World Cup of 1990, with the authorities having gone to considerable lengths to avoid keeping us in one place for too long. The aim was to do everything possible to avoid trouble – with the England yob followers still a big factor then. The England squad was easily the most travelled of all the teams in the tournament.

Did I say "uneventful?" Well, the drive through the big city of Cagliari, through which we had to go before reaching Pula, was certainly an experience, if not eventful. There were, it seemed, simply no rules of the road here. We had been serenely travelling through all this beautiful countryside when suddenly we were pitched into this great big city with cars and motor bikes whizzing around us here, there and everywhere. Remember, too, that we were in a totally strange city, frantically trying to follow directions, with limited signage for Pula and obviously no Satnav in those days. This all lasted 40 minutes or so before we were out the other side, and it was a bit of a nightmare, to be honest. The sweat certainly poured once more!

We found the hotel easily enough and then it was a case of dispatching all the players' baggage to their correct rooms and villas, in accordance with the full manifest in my possession. There was a villa for me, too – just 20 yards or so (I'm not exaggerating!) from the gorgeous white sandy beach. Just to complete the sense of paradise, I had been told in no uncertain terms that I had access to all the hotel facilities and could have absolutely anything that I wanted by way of food and drink – I just needed to sign for it, and that was it. I could even have had champagne if I wanted. (I didn't.)

This was actually the "warm-up" ahead of the main event. I was just here for a few days, sorting everything out, before I had to return to the UK on Friday, May 25 – flying back from Cagliari – for a few days' work for other clients, prior to returning to Italy for the rest of England's World Cup campaign. The players and the "various others" arrived at the Hotel Is Morus the day before I left. There was just one player missing from the squad – Chris Waddle (how we could do with him in our national team now!). He was involved in a French cup final and was following on later. So in the meantime I made arrangements for his baggage to be separately stored in the hotel.

The England party numbered around 70 in all and included players' wives and girlfriends (or the WAGS, as they later came to be known), who would be with them for this first stage of the tournament before flying home. That was 70 people whose property I had to look after! I was up at 6 am that day because I knew I had one very long and busy day ahead of me. It was a beautifully sunny start to the day – as it always seemed to be (although there was one morning when the heavens opened and I was I told that that was Sardinia's first rain for five years, repeat years!). I showered and ordered breakfast in my room. I asked for an "English" breakfast, but unfortunately their idea of this included loads of olive oil – so much so that my eggs, bacon and sausage were positively swimming in the stuff. I put that disappointment behind me and enjoyed my first fabulous dip in the warm, crystal-clear Tyrrhenian Sea. Talk about lap of luxury.

I was excited – and probably a little nervous – at the prospect of the England players arriving in the next few hours. Everything was in the right place for them – so far as I knew, all stored and double-checked – and then there they all were, at around 2 pm, piling out of the first coach to arrive. Among the instantly recognisable faces were such famous names as Gary Lineker, David Platt, Trevor Steven, Peter Beardsley, Gary Stevens, Steve Bull, and not forgetting the "daddy of them all", the late great Bobby Robson, the team manager who took England to the 1990 semi-finals and was subsequently knighted.

I stood in the main reception doorway as they disembarked – but it was not long before I had to start earning my luxurious keep. The squad included wily winger John Barnes (who had burst onto the international scene with a fabulous goal in Brazil), and it turned out that the suitcase belonging to his wife Suzie, containing loads of expensive jewellery and so on, had gone missing. A lorry had arrived separately transporting all the group's personal luggage from the airport and it had been my job to see to its distribution to all the correct rooms and villas.

It was clear that Suzie was giving John a hard time, so I said with as much conviction as I could muster: "Don't worry; it won't be far away. I'll get to the airport now and find it for you." John gave me a look as if to say: "Sorry, mate." This was my first big test and, for all my outward confidence and reassurance to Suzie, it was all a bit worrying – I simply had to find that case! I got a taxi to the airport – about half an hour's drive away – and found someone from the airline, British Airways. They checked – but reported back that nothing had been left behind.

Then they got hold of one of the chaps who had actually done the manhandling of the luggage from the aeroplane and he had explained what had happened – it turned out they had put some of the luggage onto the coach rather than the lorry. So I went back to the hotel, opened up the side panel of the coach, and with an almighty sigh of relief saw this case that was still in there together with a few other items. I pulled out the case and took it to the Barnes' room, prompting much gratitude (but alas no kiss!). John later told me: "I was so pleased when you turned up with that case – Suzie was giving me so much grief."

Everything went smoothly enough after that. It would have been about 4.30 pm when I delivered that case, and it ended a prolonged period of humping baggage around, albeit with the help of hotel porters. It had already turned into a very long day and I was starting to get tired by now and in need of a wash and refreshment – drink and food. So I headed off for a shower and a bit of a rest and then went into the bar at around 6 pm. My boss was already there – Adrian Titcombe, in charge of the FA's rules and regulations. Accompanied by his wife, he congratulated me on a good day's work.

Gordon joined us all over a drink and then he and I made our way into the restaurant for a really lovely meal. We didn't know what we were choosing – it was all in Italian, after all – but the maître de performed wonders in the way he helped us. He spoke really good English. I can't remember now what the main course was, but I do clearly recall a delightful starter, with pasta in the shape of flower heads and in a delicious tomato sauce. I hit the pillow early that night – at around 9 pm. I had had a really long day, and I knew I was flying back to London Heathrow next morning, accompanied again by Gordon, who had now completed his computer business with the Italian police and security services. You could say that I "slept for England" that night – I think I had been running on adrenalin since the previous Saturday, with nerves and excitement competing non-stop for dominance.

So much so, in fact, that for a while I had clean forgotten my gorgeous daughter Clare's second birthday! It was just before lunchtime when it struck me, and I straightaway phoned home to wish her Many Happy Returns. I apologised for not having phoned earlier. All was well - I was not in the doghouse - and I'm sure Linda would have come up trumps with a satisfactory explanation.

My flight back to the UK was with Italian Airlines and it was a really old, noisy aeroplane, with the fumes so strong you'd think you were in the back of a diesel truck. (The food and bar were good, though!) We were airborne for about three-and-a-half hours and I then caught the train from London Euston to Runcorn, bidding farewell to Gordon as he lived in London. The next day we had a lovely birthday party for Clare, made all the more special with my mum and dad also up for it.

I can't deny that my return to what I suppose you could call "the day job" was a bit of a come-down, but I was the company's only driver. They had around 30 clients, all VIP and high-profile, such as the BBC.

I flew back to Sardinia on Tuesday, June 19, but in the meantime the World Cup began 11 days earlier, and so in the interim I had to follow it all on the TV. Straightaway, in fact, there was a huge upset, with tournament favourites Argentina going down 1-0 to Cameroon. Argentina did go on to reach the final, but lost 1-0 to West Germany. The latter opened their campaign in much more promising style, beating Yugoslavia 4-1. As for England, we kicked off on June 11 with a 1-1 "bore draw" against Jack

Charlton's Ireland. That did nothing to raise our hopes – and certainly gave no hint of the drama and near-glory that were to follow.

My flight back to Italy also had the England team doctor, John Crane, among the passengers. John was a Harley Street practitioner (who died in 2009) who had four World Cups in all and was the Arsenal team doctor for some 30 years. I got to know him quite well during the tournament.

I was staying this time at the Hotel Is Molas, about a mile down the road from its sister hotel, the Is Morus, in Pula. This was another five-star, ultimate luxury job, although obviously it didn't have the sea on its doorstep (but it did have a big golf complex). I was in a room this time, rather than a villa. Here we became particularly aware of the security forces – with armed guards pacing up and down the marble floor outside my bedroom all night. Trevor Brooking, no less, would also have been very aware of this, as he was in the bedroom next to me. He was working for the BBC now and also acting as one of Bobby Robson's advisors. I didn't find it all easy to get to sleep, with the sound of those footsteps outside my door.

It was also here that I actually got to speak to Bobby Robson for the first time. I got myself all sorted in my room and then met up once more with Adrian Titcombe in the Reception area around 4 pm. He introduced me to Bobby; we shook hands and it was a great moment. I had always admired him from afar, right from his early days as Ipswich manager (when he "broke the mould" and led a little club to the old First Division championship). The reality was no disappointment. He was a really lovely fellow and put me at ease immediately. He stressed that if there was anything I needed – absolutely anything – or any way at all that he could help me, I was not to hesitate to ask him for it. I remember he was also concerned that I was the only one doing all the driving of that truck; he felt someone should have been sharing the burden. I tried to reassure him, explaining that it was no problem as this was what I was used to doing.

Next, I was introduced to Graham Kelly, who was then a year into his role as chief executive of the FA, after 11 years as its secretary. He later resigned in controversial circumstances, although an FA investigation cleared him of any wrongdoing. The contrast between this man and Bobby could hardly have been greater. His handshake was limp and sweaty – I could say I've had better handshakes with lettuce leaves - and he instantly struck me as arrogant. He was not really interested in me at all – who I was or what I was doing there. He didn't impress me one bit.

So I didn't like Graham Kelly – but it didn't bother me unduly. I had already met the great man himself – Bobby – I had had my first introductions with the players, and I was now also being introduced to other FA dignitaries, including Jack Wiseman, who also struck me as a really nice gentleman who was always glad to welcome you into his company (on which more later in this book). Jack was chairman of Birmingham City and involved with the club for more than 50 years.

That first evening at the Is Molas, I dined on my own – as I did on the second night, too. Tempting though it was, I did not want to push myself on to the players, who were in a group on the far side of the restaurant from me. I was more than happy as I was. In the mornings, I would take a swim in the 50-metre hotel pool at around 6 am and I found I had a like-minded companion in Neil Webb, the Manchester United midfielder. He was a lovely guy – big, strong and athletic, with a great sense of humour. Indeed, the players I was with were nothing like the perception we have of today's big shots, who so often seem to be unbelievably full of themselves. Bobby Robson had had this squad for some time and he had undoubtedly moulded them into a "family" of perfect gentlemen. As for Neil Webb . . . well, although I counted myself as a not-bad swimmer, there was one morning when he ended up seven lengths clear of me! (Maybe I'd had too much to drink the previous night!)

For England's second match of the tournament, on Thursday, June 21, I travelled on board the England team coach for the 30-mile trip to Cagliari, where we won 1-0 with a Mark Wright goal, which I watched from the grandstand. The trip was memorable not least for a very low-flying police helicopter escort, supplementing the police road riders. There was perceived to be a very real threat of attack by Colonel Gaddafi's forces, following the UK's air-base assistance in the United States attacks on Libya four years earlier. We gathered that the Italian special forces and our own Special Boat Services were also much in presence. One thing was for sure – the trip seemed to take forever.

For the meal back in the hotel after the match, it was the first time I was invited to sit in with the players. Paul Parker, the Fulham full-back who was on the verge of joining Manchester United (although he told me he thought he was Everton-bound), came over to me and said: "Come and join us." I didn't need any persuasion – and from then on I always dined with them. Always, it was loads of pasta; John Crane had this thing about it being so good for everyone. It must have been midnight when I had that first meal with the team. Even though it was only a 30-minute coach drive from the ground, you always had to wait for the drugs tests, and results, on two randomly-selected players after the match.

CHAPTER 16

EPIC JOURNEYS . . .
"FAME" AT LAST. . .
I MEET THE GREAT MAN . . .
AND I'M TREATED LIKE A HERO

On Saturday, June 23, we were on the move again. I had an epic journey ahead of me – a 100-mile drive to Port Torres, with a 12-hour ferry crossing to Genoa to follow. (And this time I made sure I was last, not first, onto the bally ship!) Then I was heading from Genoa to Bologna, which was another drive of eight hours. I finally arrived at our destination in the early evening – at around the same time as Argentina were recovering from their opening setback by winning 1-0 against their great South American rivals Brazil.

Thus ended a gruelling 700-mile trip. I had been driving my truck, complete with its £30,000-plus-worth of cargo, in horrendous heat - with temperatures well into the 90s for virtually the whole way. The only things I wasn't carrying for the players were their personal bags which accompanied them everywhere. But there was no immediate rest for the wicked. I now had to go through the process of unloading and dispatching all the baggage again – this time for around 50 people, with the WAGs having returned home by now.

To say I was shattered (after two days' driving in the 90s) doesn't come near it; I still don't know how I did it. Ah well, I was younger then! At least we were into another tip-top hotel now, the Novotel in Bologna. First of all, of course, I had to find it. I managed this as much as anything just by asking police officers. My truck was plastered with England World Cup imagery and wording, and so was pretty conspicuous and attention-grabbing. Everyone was so glad to see me when I pulled in at the hotel – by contrast, they had simply "hopped" up on a two-hour flight!

I took a well-earned shower and helped myself to three or four ice-cold beers and a meal – all of which, I told myself, was "fit for a hard-working famous truck driver." Why "famous?" Well, I hadn't noticed the presence of TV cameras when I unloaded my truck at the end of that marathon journey, but a friend of mine subsequently told me that I had made it on to both the 9 pm and 10 pm national news back home that night! My friend showed it all to me on video, and there was no doubting the identity of the guy hogging the centre of the pictures! They showed me unloading the truck as well as arriving in it. I was definitely a star at last! I joked that I might even make the team now – I just had to nobble Peter Beardsley or Paul Gascoigne (Gazza) first. And after all that little lot – all the travelling - I once again slept like a baby.

The next morning, I woke up to find that West Germany had suffered their first defeat, going down 2-0 to Holland, and then another treat was in store for me with my first invitation to an England training session (just to watch, not participate). This was in Bologna, but on the ground of a club from a lower league, not the senior Bologna club itself. The ground was, in fact, a bit ropey – but the session struck me as none too gruelling. It all seemed very relaxed and informal. I regarded it as quite an honour to be invited along to watch.

I mentioned Gazza just now. He was at the height of his powers and skills then, of course, long before his sad decline, and I recall how he was forever laughing and joking and winding someone up. Another clear memory is of how Trevor Steven and Gary Stephens were very much the studious types – constantly with their heads in books, learning the Italian language.

Someone else very famous who joined us, but not from the world of football, was the violinist Nigel Kennedy. As part of Italy's attempts to keep the lid on any potential trouble during the tournament, there was a total ban on alcohol being sold within a 30-mile radius for 24 hours prior to each match. Peter Beardsley had been given some 20 or 30 cases of beer by a sponsor, but he didn't drink and so he had put me in charge of the beer.

That afternoon, after attending my first training session, we all went into the TV lounge to watch Ireland beat Romania (on penalties after 0-0), and in came Mr Kennedy, who was very pally with some of the players. He said to Peter: "Anyone got any beer then?" Peter explained that you "can't get any beer anywhere," but then said to me: "James, go and get some beers." So, two trips later, I had brought down two cases of the stuff from my room. I invited the lads to help themselves, which they duly did. Luckily, Bobby Robson never came in.

Also "behind the scenes," I was very aware at this time of the unsavoury tabloid press story back home concerning Manchester United star Bryan Robson, whose World Cup hopes had been hit by injury. He had been accused in *The Sun* of having a fling with a waitress in Sardinia – a claim which was subsequently accepted as being without a grain of truth. I never got to meet Bryan. He came out with the squad but never played, flying home early.

I was back at another training session with the lads on the morning of their next match, against Belgium. There were some FA dignitaries present and they asked me to join them in having their photo taken standing inside a goalmouth. Ah well, whatever takes your fancy, I guess! But I did regard it as something of an honour to be allowed in to share the world of these old farts!

That night was a great one for England, with David Platt scoring a spectacular late winner from a long Gazza free-kick. I'm not sure, but I think this was the one that resulted in Bobby Robson being filmed dancing a jig on the touchline. (What a lovely, lovely man he was.) I had reached the ground on the team coach, once again, but then had to make my separate way to my seat in the stand – and that seat turned out to be slap bang in the middle of a party of Belgian players' wives!

We struck up some good banter, but it was the weirdest of atmospheres around me as I jumped out of my seat, cheering Platty's goal, while all around me those women were shocked into stunned silence. The main body of the England fans cheered their hearts out – on the other side of the ground from me. It was a fantastic result – especially after our overall performance, which by general consent had been pretty poor. At times the Belgians had even looked as if they were going to beat us.

Something else that made a lasting impression on me in Italy was the jaw-dropping quality of the stadiums. This was a good few years before all the grounds of the clubs in our top divisions back home became ultra-modern and comfortable. Here in Italy the stadiums I went to for the England matches were all so modern, spacious and clean. This applied to all aspects – the seating, the bars and catering, the toilets, the exit points and so on. And everything was so efficient and orderly. You didn't have to queue for ages for your coffee, for instance, as you still had to do back in England. Let it be said - the Italians really did make a great job of their World Cup.

After our Belgian triumph, we were on the move yet again the next morning, this time to a little place called Vietri sul Mare, which meant that I was driving back from the north to way down south again, almost to Naples Bay. It was yet another 700-mile journey in sweltering heat. Vietri sul Mare was about a quarter of a mile up a mountain and we were once again ushered into a stunning hotel with the kind of luxury and service with which we had now become familiar.

I had been warned to be extremely careful in Naples, which had a reputation as a violent city with a high rate of crime and muggings. With the England logo plastered all over my truck, this was one time when I would have been happier not being so "famous." In the event, there was just the one disturbing incident. The roads were toll affairs, and this is where I felt particularly vulnerable because you always had to queue to get through the booths. While you were queuing, anything could happen.

At the last toll booth on the outskirts of Naples, I found myself in one such queue. I was in an "avenue," with lines of bollards on either side, and I noticed three young lads, each with a bag, on one side, just standing there. Then I saw them walking towards me and I wound my window up to almost shut. They made out that they wanted to sell me some stuff at the side of the road. I shook my head vigorously and said I was not interested. At this, they became loud-mouthed and banged their hands against the side of my truck, trying to force me to open the door.

I had no mobile phone then, remember – if I had, I could no doubt have summoned help in no time. I managed to make slow progress, nudging along towards the booth, but still these yobs banged on my vehicle. They even tried to yank open my door. So, wisely or otherwise, I wound my window down again and gave one of them a right smack on the side of his head. I hastily re-closed the window, kept it shut and the doors locked, until I reached the booth, paid the attendant, and shot away as fast as I could. I left the youngsters in my wake, still shouting what were no doubt

118

obscenities in my direction. No-one else in the vicinity showed the slightest interest in the incident or any inclination to help me.

The motorway skirted Naples, so I did not have to face the threat of any trouble in the city itself. As I drove up and down the mountains, it was a scene of utter splendour – as was so often the case throughout my time in that beautiful country. And I didn't even have any difficulty finding the hotel. I simply stopped and asked a couple at the roadside. They only turned out to be English tourists, didn't they, who regularly came here for their holidays and knew exactly where the hotel was!

So once again I arrived at a hotel, with my truck, totally shattered. And once again I had to spend a further one-and-a-half hours loading and dispatching before I could finally stop. Then I went to Reception to find out how late they would carry on serving dinner, because first I needed to freshen up with a shower - only for Adrian Titcombe to come through and insist that I went straight into the restaurant for my meal. I said I simply had to get washed first, but he was adamant. "No, no, don't worry," he said, "just get yourself in here for a meal; you've earned it."

So I followed him in – and received a standing ovation from everyone! All the players, dignitaries and various others stood up and applauded me heartily. That was the most amazing moment for me and I don't suppose I have ever felt more elated – or embarrassed! I duly sat down, stinking and feeling very dishevelled, ready for my evening meal, and no-one batted an eyelid regarding my state. Everyone was just so pleased to see me, it seemed, and to know that all the baggage had arrived safely. They had appreciated what a tough journey I had just completed.

After another two hours, I was able to talk myself away from the restaurant, have that long overdue shower and a much-needed drink or two. And I was not so tired that I couldn't go back down again later that evening for a disco in the hotel!

CHAPTER 17

LIFE JUST GETS
BETTER AND BETTER . . .
AND ENGLAND REACH
THE SEMI-FINALS!

We were at Vietri sul Mare for five days, and during this time I got to know David Bloomfield, son of Jimmy Bloomfield, the BBC radio commentator and former Blackpool, Everton and England footballer. David was the person who organised the hotel bookings. This was a particularly important issue once England had reached the qualifying stages of the tournament, as obviously you could not book well in advance because you did not know whether England would still be in the tournament and who they would be playing. Sometimes it would be the morning of departure before I knew exactly where we were heading next!

A couple of memories spring to mind from the morning after the Belgium triumph. I was sitting in the hotel's reception-cum-lounge area, reading an English newspaper that someone had left behind, with David Platt and several other players close by, when in breezed Gazza wearing Union Jack shorts! That just about summed him up. Life was never dull – and usually instantly brighter – whenever he was around. What was it Bobby Robson called him – "daft as a brush!" In years to come, Gazza freely described Bobby as like a second father to him – and revealed that he had cried his eyes out for three hours on learning of his death in 2009.

Shortly after Gazza had "done his thing" that morning, one of the hotel guests came up to me and asked me for my autograph! (I know I had been on TV, but this was ridiculous!) I tried to explain that I was not a player, but with no success. Platty saw what was happening and said quietly to me, behind my "fan's" back, "just sign." He was right, of course, as it was easier just to sign rather than risk confusion and maybe even offence. I ended up supplying my autograph for loads of people after that! Maybe some of them thought afterwards: "Who the ---- is 'James Maloney?'" Or even: "Well, one day he may become famous, and we will already have his autograph." *Dream on, James!*

The next match was not until the Sunday, with longer gaps now between the fixtures as the tournament progressed. So we enjoyed a relaxed little spell – pottering around the hotel, taking in some sights, sitting around the pool with a beer, and enjoying a long lunch! Nothing was ever rushed. It was a lovely way of life.

At Thursday teatime, I met a man who was going to be our coach driver, employed by Italia 90, an Italian called Gussepe or Seppe. Instead of dining with the players in the hotel that evening, I went out with Seppe for a meal together at a local restaurant. We got quite pally. The restaurant was built into a cliff and, I learnt, owned by his uncle. We got there after wandering around and having a drink or two. The restaurant had a rustic interior, with wooden tables and candles, and I remember ordering a pizza that was absolutely delicious. It was the first time since I had been in Italy that I had had a proper pizza! (None of the others had been to my taste at all, to put it mildly.) We also shared a bottle of some lovely dry white wine from a local vineyard.

As we dined, people kept coming up to our table and shaking our hands, being introduced to me as friends and acquaintances of either Seppe or his uncle. I was feeling so good that I told Seppe: "This evening is on me," but he was shocked at that and said: "No, no, you are my guest – I am paying." It was a battle of wills – or so I thought – and I took the opportunity to grab a waiter and ask for the bill. That bill, though, never arrived. It turned out that neither of us was paying – it had all been taken care of by Seppe's uncle! I would love to have gone back to that great little restaurant before we moved on, but I decided against it as I feared it might have looked as if I was expecting another free meal!

The Friday morning saw another "first" for me. I went into Naples with the squad, to a much better club ground than the last one for their training session – and they invited me to join them for a kick-about! Life was just getting better and better. I think it was Peter Beardsley who asked me in, and I remember him saying to Gazza: "Watch this Maloney guy. Watch him if he kicks you – he's after your place!" That was a fun hour, all right, just kicking the ball about among ourselves. Gazza would mess with you and it was good fun trying to get the ball off him.

Now I was well and truly "in" with the World Cup squad! I felt totally at ease with them; I could speak to them without feeling shy or pushy; I was very much on the inside now! As bonus, there was also a very attractive – and almost certainly seriously rich – lady in her 40s (I was 32) who took a considerable interest in me at this hotel. We got on well and I enjoyed her company, with no shortage of ribbing from the players as a result – but for the record let me state categorically, with hand firmly on heart, that "nothing ever came of it!"

The next day, Saturday, was a bit of an adventure for me. Against all advice, I left the camp after lunch and wandered up the mountain, on my own, through little villages until I eventually reached the highest village of them all. It would have been about 2.30 pm by now and I quickly saw that the community included one tiny public bar. I ventured in there, being very much in need of a beer after my energy-sapping climb in the customary heat. There were just two other drinkers there, along with one person behind the bar. I asked for a beer, mindful of the cost of a bottle of Perrioni back in the hotel – around £3 in English money. Here it was all of 50 pence!

Half-way through that first beer, I was very mindful that still no-one had spoken to me, apart from the barman telling me the cost of my drink. The other two had just carried on drinking and chatting among themselves, ignoring me. Well, I'm a stubborn bugger and I thought: "Okay, I've not exactly been made to feel very welcome in this place, but there's no way I'm just going to walk into it and out of it again." So as soon as I had drained my glass, I promptly ordered another.

I was about ten minutes into my second beer when some more people came in. That was when the mood seemed to change. They began talking to me, asking what I was doing up there in that village (which must have been about a mile above sea level). I had learnt to speak a bit of Italian by now, so I made the effort to communicate with them in their own language. A bit. Next thing I knew, the barman was sending someone off into the village to fetch a resident who could speak English quite well. This gentleman joined us and the mood really took off. I explained more precisely why I was in Italy, spelling out my involvement with the England World Cup squad, but adding that I was very keen to sample some company with "the proper people of Italy."

This clearly pleased them and the beer began to flow - and I didn't have to pay for any of it. The bar gradually filled to capacity and after a while it seemed as though everyone in this little village had turned out to meet me. Some asked if I could get tickets for matches, and it pained me to explain that this was outside my powers, adding that the tickets for myself only reached me at the last minute. We chatted football incessantly – with them naturally betting on an Italian win in the World Cup Final and me forecasting an English success – and it went on like this all afternoon.

It was a great experience. And to think: when I arrived, no-one had spoken to me, but when I left it seemed as if the whole village had shaken my hand. I did not really want to leave, but duty called, of course, and so I staggered back down that mountain! I joined the England players again to watch that evening's World Cup action on TV – with Ireland losing 1-0 to Italy in the quarter-final. That was it – "my" Jack Charlton and his over-achieving boys were on their way home. (On the same evening, Argentina continued their progress with a 1-0 win over Yugoslavia.)

At dinner that evening, I told the players about my afternoon adventure up the mountain. I subsequently learnt that Bobby Robson was none too pleased when he got to hear about it, as it had been expressly against advice, but as I had come back safe and sound he evidently decided to make nothing of it. Nothing was ever said about it.

I went down to the disco again that evening for an hour or so, as did several of the players. But most tended to do their own thing in the evenings – some went out into Vietri sul Mare. I remember Paul Parker returning with a stunning brand new white suit that he had bought. He had a big thing about clothes, and suits in particular. He always had to be immaculate. His appearance in this suit now made me think of gangster characters in *The Godfather* film!

The next day, a new month dawned – July 1 – and now it was time for action once more with England's quarter-final match against Cameroon that evening in Naples. It was another gloriously sunny start to the day, which rapidly became very hot, and excitement in the camp was now at fever pitch; everyone knew we were in for a really tough match against one of the tournament's outstanding teams.

After a light training session in the morning, the orders had been given for everyone – all the players – to go to bed, or at least their bedrooms, for the afternoon. I remember how the place seemed utterly dead for that time, and I was just plain bored! I could not sleep, so I ended up just sitting beside the pool and watching the clock go round. Things began to come to life again at 4 pm, when the players re-emerged for a light meal.

For the 30-mile coach trip into Naples, I sat at the front near to our driver, Seppe, and the journey once again seemed to take forever, with loads of stops and starts orchestrated by our heavy police escort. The atmosphere on board was just fantastic. Everyone (outwardly at least) was very relaxed and the jokes flew around non-stop. Some of the players took the mickey out of the police out-riders, likening them to "the Keystone cops."

For this match, I at least didn't find myself camped in amongst "the enemy." This time I was seated with various other people from the English FA, more or less on the half-way line. It was a big stadium and the crowd noise was fantastic. The match totally lived up to its expectations. It was a breathtakingly exciting encounter, with England emerging 3-2 winners. We had made it into the semi-finals! This was the furthest the team had gone since famously winning the World Cup in 1966.

As per usual, we had to wait in the coach for a good hour or more afterwards while the random drugs tests were carried out and the results assessed – I think the lucky two this time were Gazza and Gary Lineker. The heat was still a big factor, even at this time of night, and the coach doors were left open. Fans – English and Italian – were surrounding our coach and the Cameroon one, albeit with rings of police in between.

All of a sudden we were aware of a commotion as a guy who I would guess was in his 30s, wearing beige slacks and T-shirt and with a crucifix around his neck, managed to break through the police cordon and board our coach. He was immediately jumped on and grabbed hold of by myself, Adrian Titcombe and Les Walker (the FA's head of security), who had all been sat at the front of the coach. We had no idea who or what he was and were not prepared to take any chances, with the Gaddafi threat still fresh in our minds.

The police joined us in seconds, but it turned out that the intruder, an Italian, was not really a threat of any kind. He was just a huge fan of England's goalkeeper, Peter Shilton, who was regarded by many as the world's No. 1

at that time. This guy had taken a big risk – he really could have been shot, as the Italian police were known to be very trigger-happy. The police wanted to eject him, but we persuaded them to let him stay for a few minutes – everyone, after all, was in a great mood now after the win.

We called Peter Shilton down from the back of the coach because it was apparent that the fan just wanted to shake his hand. Peter went one better – going back to his seat and then returning with a pair of his goalkeeper's gloves as a souvenir for him. "These are the ones I played with tonight," he said as he handed them over. At this, the tears flooded down the fan's face. He shook his hand as if he would never let go of it – and then said "this is for you," as he took off his crucifix. "No, no, no," Peter protested, "there's no need for that."

At this point, Les Walker intervened and advised: "Peter, I think you're going to have to take it or else he's going to be offended." The "deal" was done and the two men hugged each other – and for me that was one of the most moving moments of the entire tournament. Make that my whole footballing life. Mission accomplished, our uninvited guest was finally ushered off the coach by the police. The coach pulled away, we returned to our hotel, and the celebrations duly went on into the early hours of the morning. There was also a lot of noise coming from outside our hotel that night, I can tell you!

We had a late meal in the hotel and I remember saying to Paul Parker "Well done, mate, you had a great game." "Thanks for that, James, I appreciate it," he replied. Eventually – and I've really no idea what time it was – Bobby ruled: "That's enough now, lads – bed time, please."

The following day, we were heading off to our next camp, for the semi-final against West Germany. It was another 800-mile epic and we were bound back up north again, this time for the famous wine region of Asti.

Press conference in Turin. Table line-up includes Bobby Robson, David Platt, Mark Wright and Trevor Brooking.

Boarding the team coach for the semi-final against West Germany. Just about to get on are Paul Gascoigne and Tony Dorigo.

Jonathan King (centre) outside the Juventus stadium.
I think the Rolls Royce on the left was his!

Party time after the semi-final.
Me with David Bloomfield (left) and Neil Webb.

Neil Webb, right, appears to be tiring as New Order join him at the party after the semi-final.

Left to right, facing camera – Neil Webb, Steve Bull, Chris Waddle, unrecalled.

Me with my future Leeds United team mate (haha),
Tony Dorigo

"Wing wizard" John Barnes in Bari, with Paul Clarke, a clerk with European & General Shipping

Historic homes. The trulli in Alberobello.

In demand! Big crowds at the entrance to the England team's hotel in Alberobello.

CHAPTER 18

"CAN LIFE GET ANY BETTER THAN THIS . . . ?"

What lay just round the corner was the second most important match in the history of English soccer – and I had the supreme privilege of being right at the heart of it. Only one match – before or since – had ranked higher than the upcoming semi-final against Germany, and that was the final itself back in 1966, which England won.

We had been camped in the Naples Bay area for five days and I had fallen in love with its beauty, its panoramic views and its friendly people. It was simply stunning and – World Cup semi-final or no World Cup semi-final – I found myself feeling very reluctant to leave it! To be honest, just about everywhere we had stayed was incredibly beautiful, but this had been very much the jewel in the crown. One day I hope to return there – with my wife Gail. In fact, I've promised her that we will! (Trouble is, there always seem to be so many other places we want to go!)

But for now – in that never to be forgotten summer of 1990 – it was back on to the road once more, and another drive of around 800 miles in the scorching heat. You were talking midday temperatures well in the 90s, with unrelenting sunshine from dawn to dusk, day after day. I set off once more in my 3.5-ton Avico truck at 3 am with all the gear – all the personal luggage, food and medical supplies for the squad, the coaching staff, the officials and various "hangers-on." The party totalled 52.

(The food part involved all the sauces, mustard, beans and so on from back home that the players had wanted to have with them. I would deliver it to the kitchen wherever we were staying, and these things would then be available to our party in addition to everything else on the menu. My duties also included laying out each player's training kit beside the door to his room. I did that every day.)

It was a long day ahead – a VERY long day – and I would be shattered by the end of it. At least, there was the prospect of an easier final leg of the journey than I had been accustomed to. Usually, I had no idea exactly where our hotel was in each new location, and there was no Satnav then, of course. This could be quite a worry, and as much as anything I relied on winding down my windows and seeking the help of English-looking tourists – who could speak my language and who I hoped would already be fairly familiar with the place. This actually worked quite well. (It was not difficult to spot such people – they generally stood out like a sore thumb!)

For the semi-final, though, I had no such concerns. Our base was to be a hotel that formed part of the huge state-of-the-art Hasta training complex for the mighty Juventus, one of the world's all-time most famous football clubs. These days, England "has it all" in terms of modern stadiums with every conceivable facility, but back in the 1990s we still had diddly-squit in that direction . . . and here was a complex that definitely belonged to the next century! It just took your breath away. Together with our luxury hotel, there was a vast array of training pitches, gymnasia, tennis courts, restaurant and bar . . . all in the heart of wine country. Couldn't be bad, eh!

But first I had to get there, to Asti - with another 800-mile marathon trek. And the hardest – or potentially most threatening – part was at the start, with the little matter of getting through the city of Naples. This was – and still is – notorious for its "bandit territory" status. You had to have your wits about you at all times and – this was the golden rule that you ignored at your peril – on no account did you stop, for anybody! I had been well briefed on what to expect. It was nothing unusual, for instance, to come across someone apparently lying injured in the middle of the road, only to discover it was a ghastly set-up as you stopped to help. If the guy was genuinely hurt, that was just his bad luck – you had to drive on.

In the event, all went well for me – it was at dead of night, after all – and I took a break for breakfast at a transport café at around 8 am. Thoughts of an English-style fry-up entered my mind . . . but no such luck! Instead of baked beans, bacon and eggs, it was a case of cheese and tomato baggette. But it was very enjoyable for all that, along with the coffee. And the place itself would have left our own transport cafes standing. The Europeans do things with so much more style, don't they? In this case, someone coming in dressed in a suit and tie would not have looked or felt out of place.

Four hours later, it was time for another transport café, this time for some lunch, and I was now just 140 miles away from my destination. I was confident that I would be there before the players. That's what I always liked to do, if possible, but they were flying up and so I didn't know exactly when to expect them. I was also conscious of the fact that they had beaten me to it for our arrival in Vietri sul Mare – which was not good when you remember that I had all their things.

I was eating my snack lunch in the truck – I always left it unguarded for as short a time as possible – when I glanced in a wing mirror and noticed around a dozen people approaching my vehicle from the rear and down one side. I straightaway went into defence mode, making sure the doors were locked and getting ready to drive off fast. But then I realised that they were wearing England football shirts. So I left the doors locked but lowered my driver's window slightly. At this point, you need to remember that my truck had the words "England Football Team Transport" emblazoned all over it in big letters. This was what European and General Shipping, my employers – the owners of the truck and the suppliers of the service – had wanted, but from a security point of view I was never happy with that and I can tell you that Bobby Robson most certainly wasn't!

Anyway, on this occasion it turned out I had no need to worry. The approaching group of England fans were perfectly genuine. They had given in to curiosity; they wanted to know who I was and whether the coach with all the players was anywhere nearby. Alas, I couldn't please them on that score, but they then asked me all sorts of questions – where were the team staying, was anyone injured, did I know the line-up for the Germany match? They were a good bunch and I wished I could have spent more time chatting with them, but I had a plan – a schedule - and I wanted to stick to it. Before setting off again, I gave them all some memorabilia which they loved – team photographs, key rings, trinkets and so on. I had been given loads of these by the FA for just such situations or to help dilute any threats. The faces on these fans were an absolute picture as I handed out this largesse.

I pulled into Asti and discovered yet another beautiful, clean town, this one with a population of around 70,000. I said just now that this one was easy to find; it was even easier for the fact that it was just off the motorway, close to the toll gate. I went to reception, where I learnt that all the squad's rooms were ready but that they – the England party – were not due until around 6 pm. "Great," I thought, "that gives me time to sort things out."

I made for my own room and enjoyed a much-needed shower. Also much-needed by now was a nice bottle of ice-cold beer. Now then, in your wildest dreams, can you begin to imagine how, in these circumstances, after driving the best part of 12 hours in searing heat, I would manage to take one-and-a-half hours to sink that first thirst-quenching beer? It's because, to my surprise, I met Trevor Brooking at the bar, that's how.

He was sitting there, sipping a cup of coffee, and greeted me warmly as I joined him. "You've got here safe, then, and I see you've done well to make it so soon," he said. Although I didn't realise it at the time, Trevor was going to be a co-commentator for the BBC on the big match. He proceeded to talk football . . . and talk and talk and talk, and he had me spellbound, hanging on his every word. His inside knowledge of the game was phenomenal. But first I had to order my drink, a bottle of Peroni beer. The order was taken by a petite, dark-haired Chinese Italian barmaid, Lou-anne, who was such a stunner that I have always thought of her, and referred to her, ever since as the "vision of beauty." I became quite friendly with her, and I was so struck by her appearance and personality that we seriously discussed arrangements for her to come over to Britain and work as nanny to our two children – for myself and Linda, my first wife – but in the event nothing came of that. I can still see her cute little face even now, so vividly, bless her.

My intention was to down that first beer in a flash and move quickly on to the next one, and then a third, before returning to the business of the day ahead with the arrival of the England party. As I say, though, it ended up pretty warm beer! I wish I could have recorded that chat with Trevor. It was the most fascinating conversation – albeit one-way! – that I had ever had. I have lived and breathed football since the age of five and have talked to some of the greatest players of the age. In short, I thought I knew "everything" about the greatest game on earth, but by the time Trevor finished talking it felt more as if I had previously known nothing about it. His knowledge was fantastic; his tactical know-how (as a former West Ham United and England midfield maestro) was something else altogether.

He just left me awestruck. Struck by such knowledge and wisdom, I asked him why on earth he had never pursued a career in football management; I felt sure he would have been a huge success. But that just wasn't for him, he replied. There was too much stress in that direction – and club chairmen did not have enough respect for their managers. Instead, Trevor was quite content with his life as a pundit and with the cardboard box business that he had in the east end of London - not far from Bethnal Green tube station.

(This was an area I knew well. I used to sup a regular pint or three there with a good mate, Steve Cornish – who was actually an East Ender. One of our regular drinking holes was the Blind Beggar, which is where the notorious Ronnie Kray shot and killed fellow criminal George Cornell in front of witnesses, in 1966.)

For Italia 90, as I recall, Trevor was not involved with the England party in any official capacity. However, as well as his TV commentating, he was also acting as something of an unofficial scout by watching our competitors. He has gone on to do so much for England, and football in general, since then, of course. He is such a gentleman, such a great ambassador for the game. I count myself truly honoured to have known him. When he left that bar for his room, and a shower ahead of the England party's arrival, I looked down at my bottle and was genuinely shocked to discover that I had consumed all of one mouthful of that beer! I dawdled for a few minutes longer, reflecting on all that Trevor had told me and feeling excited at just how optimistic he was that England would win the World Cup. If I had had any doubts before, they had been banished out of sight; I definitely felt the same way now!

"Brilliant," I thought, as I looked out of the window at the gorgeous Piedmont countryside, "just brilliant. It doesn't – can't – get any better than this." My "life with the stars" had not gone unnoticed back home, either. Even before the whole thing had started, the *Liverpool Echo* had carried a page lead story and photo of me, with the headline TRUCKER GEARS UP FOR ENGLAND, and the sub-heading: Lucky Jim Is Picked For World Cup Squad. The article read:--

Even before England boss Bobby Robson has announced his World Cup squad, there's one name already on the team sheet. Merseyside's Jim Maloney will join the nation's top soccer stars in Sardinia and will be hoping to steer them on the road to success. He's checked into the team's hotel and will be a key member of the England set-up.

Because Jim is driving the truck that holds England's soccer strips, food, medical supplies, spare pairs of boots and even 28 personalised sets of golf clubs! The 32-year-old trucker, who reveals he was a tricky right winger in his amateur playing days, leaves the Liverpool depot of EGS plc in Speke tomorrow to drive to England's Cagliari base.

"I got a bit of stick from my mates when they found out I was joining the England party," said Jim, "but I told them I was taking my boots along, just in case Peter Beardsley fails a late fitness test." Jim, who lives in Runcorn, will drive through Dover, Calais, France's Mont Blanc Tunnel, and Genoa before arriving in Cagliari on May 24.

Alan Dee, projects director for European and General Shipping, said England's World Cup contract was no problem for the company. "We've just handled all Great Britain's gear at the New Zealand Commonwealth Games and we're getting set for the 1992 Olympics in Barcelona," he said.

The reality did indeed live up to the dream, and then some, but life can occasionally kick you in the teeth just when you least expect it and when everything seems to be going along just a little too well. Little did I realise, as I reflected on that chat with Trevor Brooking and looked out across that stunning training complex, that in a few short hours' time I would receive some shattering bad news.

CHAPTER 19

THE MOOD IS SHATTERED WITH
THE LOSS OF DEAR LITTLE ANNA

The England party arrived in Asti shortly after 6 pm and they were all directed to the right rooms, with the right belongings, with no hitches. I was having a chat with Dave Bloomfield in the reception area when Bobby Robson came up to me, offered his hand, and asked if I had had a good journey. "Yes," I said, "and I managed to have a great conversation with Trevor Brooking before you arrived. You know what, Bobby, he knows nearly as much as you and I do about football!" He laughed loudly at that, as did David and Don Howe.

Then Bobby added: "See you in the restaurant, James, and thanks again for looking after us all; I'm really grateful to have you in my team." With that, he walked off to his room – and I thought, what a great guy. "Did you hear what he said?" I asked David. "Yes," he replied. "Well done, James."

I returned to my room for another shower ahead of the evening meal. Before going into the restaurant, I decided to take a relaxing stroll around the training ground. What a beautiful evening, I thought, as I wandered over to the football pitch where I knew the great Juventus trained – and where, just days ago, Brazil had trained prior to knocking Argentina out of this World Cup tournament. I wondered who had been in my room immediately before me. Maybe it was Dunga . . . or Ze-carlos . . . or Carlos Mozer (who was a friend of our own Chris Waddle.)

I looked forward to joining the England lads in a kickabout on this pitch the next morning. Well, I hoped I could. I never asked – never tried to impose myself on them - but they usually invited me. That was my way – politeness, good manners – and I have always believed that people respect you for that. But all that – my next kickaround – could wait for now. I headed back into the hotel and made for the bar for a pre-meal drink and another chat with the Vision Of Beauty.

Dinner was a meal fit for a World Cup footballer and maybe even for a king himself. Or that's how it seemed. The main course was a divine fish dish with pasta and salad garnish, beautifully presented and laid out, in one of the best hotel restaurants in Asti. One thing we were never short of at our meals was tagretelli – the dreaded pasta. Dr Crane swore by it, insisting that we always started our meals with it. It became a standing joke whenever we were telling someone what we had had to eat; it always ended with " . . . and tagretelli!" I liked it, actually, but everyone got a bit fed up with it after a while, night after night after night. Still, if it had helped us reach the semi-final of the World Cup . . . !

The mood was really good; the banter was great and Paul Gascoigne – Gazza – was truly in his element as an entertainer. If he hadn't made it as a footballer, a career on stage could surely have beckoned. As for me, I remember going over to Peter Beardsley and saying: "I'm going to tell Bobby to pick you for Wednesday (the Germany match) because I can't play myself due to an old injury!" David Platt overheard that and urged me: "Don't do that. We want you in our team, and Peter can do your job! We might just beat the Germans if you're in the team." "Okay," I said. "I'll give Peter the keys to my truck." Then I instructed Peter: "Make sure you tell Dr Crane that we're out of pasta!"

How I miss those meal times – breakfast, lunch and dinner. I guess we were as close as it gets among football squads to being one big happy family. Bobby had certainly done his stuff in knitting us together; he had scored a huge hit in that direction. At the risk of repeating myself, it was such a privilege and an honour to have been a part of it all. I was lapping up some very special moments – again and again.

It was around 11 pm when Don Howe managed to get everyone to their rooms. I sat on the edge of my bed and suddenly realised how tired I was – make that exhausted. I had, after all, been on the go since 3 am that morning. I guess the adrenalin must have kept me going. What a day that had been, I reflected, as I drifted off to sleep.

I slept like a baby, not stirring at all, and woke up at 6.30 am the next day, Tuesday, July 3 – the last day before the BIG ONE! I lay on the bed for ten minutes or so, just thinking about things and wondering what this day had in store for me. I contemplated strolling into Asti and wondered who might like to join me. I loved looking around new places – playing the tourist. And these Italian towns and cities were something else, full of character and history, with some stunning architecture and a very real sense of timelessness. The players would be training from 10 am to midday, so my stroll would have to be after lunch.

So I showered and put on my England training kit – I was replacing Peter Beardsley, after all, haha – but alas, my mood would very shortly be turned upside down. After breakfast, I was talking with Adrian Titcombe – checking that everything was in order and asking if there was anything else he needed from me – when the hotel receptionist interrupted: "Excuse me, Signor Maloney, there is an urgent telephone call for you from England. I will put it through to your room."

Straightaway, as I headed for my room, I knew something was very seriously wrong. I had been in regular touch with home. Whenever I had chance, I would ring Mum and tell her where I was and what I was doing, leaving my hotel phone number in case of emergency. I would also phone Linda and Gail, my friend and future wife.

I was in a panic as I entered my room and lifted the telephone receiver. It was Mum, who said: "Sit down, James, I've got some bad news for you." I was already sitting, ready for the bombshell. "Is it Dad?" I asked, knowing that he was no longer in the best of health.

"No," she replied. "It's Anna."

"What's wrong with Anna?"

"She died last night."

You could have hit me with a baseball bat and the pain would not have compared with what I felt at that moment, hearing those four terrible words. Anna was the seven-year-old daughter of my favourite cousin Robert and his wife Katie. She was Robert's pride and joy and had been one of our bridesmaids just three years earlier. I was stunned. I managed to ask what had happened exactly, and Mum explained that Anna, who had two brothers, Robert and Steven, had suffered a brain haemorrhage.

I was devastated by her death. I felt supreme sympathy for her parents in their loss . . . and, being so far away, I felt utterly helpless. You torture yourself at such times; it dawned on me that while I had been eating and drinking and chatting and joking, poor little Anna had been dying. I was shaking . . . I felt so selfish, although I subsequently realised, of course, that that was silly. It hadn't been my fault, but I reckon most people in my position would have felt the same. Tears were streaming down my face. I had only seen her 12 weeks earlier, at Easter, when I was up in Berwick-Upon-Tweed for four days. It just seemed impossible that she had now passed away, and so suddenly. Even writing this now, some 34 years later, brings a big lump to my throat. There just seems no sense or reason for such a thing happening. The word "why" invades my mind again and again. She would have been 40 now, maybe with a family of her own. What a tragic loss of life.

Shock paralysed me. After about half an hour, there was a knock on the door; it was David Bloomfield telling me they were setting off for training and was I coming? My face said it all. "James, what's wrong?" he asked. I told him, and said I would not be at training. He said he would let Adrian know, and with that he left me alone. I returned to sit on my bed; I really didn't know what to do. Should I ask Adrian if I could go back to England or should I stay and see the job through?

Two more hours passed and then there was another knock on the door. This time it was Bobby and Adrian – dear Lord, what lovely guys they were – and I told them to come in. They were great about it. Adrian said he would arrange to get me on the next flight home and Bobby stressed: "No-one will blame you or think any the worse of you if you decide to go home."

I made an instant decision. "Bobby . . . Adrian . . . I'm going to see it through," I said. "You and everyone here are doing their job and I'm going to do mine." At this, they looked at each other – and they knew I meant it. "Right," said Bobby, "let's start by getting some lunch."

"I'll be a few minutes," I replied. "I've just got to phone Mum and wash my face and then I'll be down." When I joined them for lunch, it was soon apparent that everyone was aware by now of my tragic news, and they were all very sympathetic. Back home, Mum and Dad were agreed that there was nothing I could do and they had no problem with my decision to stay on. They were leaving Cornwall for Berwick-Upon-Tweed the next day.

After lunch, I got on with the job – handing out the kit for a one-hour light training session – and then went into Asti. It was a beautiful town – not least the bank I went into. This had gorgeous marble floors and it was almost like being in a church – it was all very quiet, with people talking to each other virtually in whispers. There were no glass barriers at the cash desks. It was all very open and very different from what I was used to in Britain. I pondered that maybe Italy didn't have any bank robbers!

Then I found myself passing a café and I noticed three riggers from BBC TV sitting outside. I had already met them a few times during the tournament. They invited me to join them. I hesitated for a moment and then thought "why not?" I never mentioned my preoccupation with my tragic news from back home – there was no point in spoiling their afternoon. These three lads were as excited as everyone else about the next day's big match. And – also like everyone else, it seemed – they were convinced that we would be heading to Rome for the final, and that we would be lifting the World Cup.

I eventually returned to the hotel in time for an hour's lie-down prior to dinner. What I liked about the meal schedule in Italy was that the meals were so unrushed. Dinner was very much an event and would typically last anything up to three hours! I left my room for the restaurant and pledged to myself: "I'm not going to be gloomy; I don't want everyone to feel awkward towards me."

I was met at the restaurant by Don Howe, who asked: "You okay, James." "Yes thanks, Don," I replied. "I'm not going to have a gloomy face." He smiled and said: "Okay. . . . oh and by the way, you're at our table tonight. Bobby asked me to tell you that you're his guest." So I joined Don and Bobby, along with Trevor Brooking, Mike Kelly, the assistant coach, and Bert Millichip, who was chairman of the FA at that time.

Millichip . . . now there was a man I truly did not like. I know it's bad form to speak ill of the dead (he died in 2002), but to omit the following would render this account of my Italia 90 experience as incomplete and not entirely honest. I despised the man after the way I heard him talking about one of my all-time heroes – the LATE Don Revie, former Leeds United and England manager. I despised Millichip all the more – lost all respect for him - for that fact that Revie was no longer around to defend himself. Millichip never missed a chance to run down Revie, who had died a year earlier. To me, Don Revie was ten times the man Millichip ever was. Not least because he had played for England six times. The best "the weazle" – as I called Millichip – could manage in his playing career was West Bromwich Albion's third team. Some claim to fame!

Unfortunately, my dinner table now was shared with three guys who were clearly good friends of his, so I had to keep my tongue bitten whenever I felt like telling Millichip what I thought of him – which was not easy, given the strong temptation! What really stuck in my gullet more than anything – as I saw him tucking into his free nosh – was that neither he, nor, I believe, anyone else from the FA, had attended Don Revie's funeral. It struck me that the FA's hierarchy had been so full of their own importance that they could not see further than their own noses.

Okay, my tongue was bitten this time, but earlier on I did have a run-in with Millichip, after he had been verbally tearing Revie to pieces back in Bologna. On that less formal occasion, I was able to defend Don. Millichip's dislike for my hero all seemed to stem from the controversial events in 1977 when Revie, still under contract, quit as England manager to become coach to the United Arab Emirates. This undeniably tarnished his image and reputation, but the facts of the matter were altogether rather different, as anyone who took the trouble to delve deeper into it would know.

Nothing, however – not even this Millichip ****hole – was going to detract from the excitement and pleasure now mounting ahead of the big, big match the next day. I went to my bedroom, mulled over the day's events, phoned Mum and then drifted off to sleep – maybe, for all I know, with a little dream or two of England skipper Terry Butcher lifting THAT trophy . . .

CHAPTER 20

THE BIG DAY IS FINALLY HERE

Wednesday, the 4th July 4, 1990 . . . just maybe not the best of omens for us, I reflected, as I awoke at 6 am, as per usual, to the sight of brilliant sunshine streaming through the curtains, also as per usual. Independence Day inevitably reminded me that England had suffered an inglorious 1-0 defeat at the hands of the United States back in 1950. That was England's World Cup debut, with the FA – amazingly as it seems now – having boycotted the three previous tournaments in a dispute with FIFA over payments made to amateur players. England had been heavy favourites against a hastily assembled US team composed of part-time players, but the rest, as they say, is history.

Now here we were, hoping to make history of a much more favourable kind, being just one step away from the final in Rome. "Crikey," I thought, "today's the day." But at that moment, my thoughts went straight back to Anna, and I said a little prayer for her and her family. I showered and made for the restaurant, only to find no-one else there yet. So I went for a wander around the hotel grounds. There were three groundsmen/gardeners already busy tending to the flower beds and cutting the grass on the training pitches. It was yet another beautiful, peaceful morning, and yet again I marvelled at the surrounding beauty, the warm air and the lovely fresh smell of the country in summer. Just perfect, I thought.

I looked at my watch – 6.55 am – so headed back to the restaurant. There, to my delight, I saw Dr Crane, Norman Medhurst and Fred Street, the physios, and Adrian Titcombe. Boy, did I love these guys' company. All of them had a great sense of humour; all of them were true gentlemen. They all asked if I was okay, and I told them I was, thank you. I was going to have a busy time working with these four men today, and so I had to make sure we had the right medical equipment and the right team kit laid out. Bobby wanted a light training session at 10 am, so over breakfast we discussed what had to be done. These guys were so professional, and yet the next laugh was never very far away. What sheer pleasure it was to work with them.

Talk about a "buzz." You could almost reach out and touch the excitement and, yes, the optimism pervading the whole England camp. Just before 10 am, I got an Italian newspaper and sat down with it in the hotel lounge. That's when the Vision Of Beauty rejoined me, challenging: "You can read Italian?" "Not really," I said, "I'm just trying to get a sense of what they're saying about England." I had picked up a smattering of Italian, in conversation, over the previous weeks – but reading it was much harder for me. So, with a big smile, I added: "But you can! Will you read this to me?" There was a section about that night's game and Vision Of Beauty sat down beside me and read it out. While she was doing so, Steve Bull, the England striker, walked past, looked at us both and bent down to joke: "You should save that for bedtime!"

That was a tad embarrassing, to be sure, and I began to formulate a reply in my mind, but fortunately I had sufficient wit to realise that it would probably only have made things worse – no doubt Steve would have spread the word and other players, Gazza especially, would not have been slow to take the Mickey out of me.

At the training session, I stood behind the goal, just to the left of the left post, and decided to take a photo of the action – this being the last such session before the semi-final match. I raised the camera to my eye . . . and was struck by a sharp pain shooting right through my body. It turned out Chris Waddle had taken a shot at goal from 12 yards out, missed and hit me in the ribs. (Waddle . . . missing the goal . . . from 12 yards out. Hmmm, maybe that, too, was a bad omen for England in view of what was to follow in the dramatic and heartbreaking finale to that night's match!) Chris had knocked the stuffing out of me. He duly ran over to check that I was okay and apologise. "Change your boots," I said with a forced smile. Crumbs, I thought, that hurt.

Anyway, all was well again when he and his colleagues invited me onto the pitch once more to join them in a kickabout at the end of the training session. That was quite something, in fact; here I was, playing with the England football team, just hours before one of the most important matches in the nation's history, and one which would be watched by many millions around the globe. Then we left the training pitch and headed back for lunch – including, yes, yet more tagretelli!

Afterwards, the players went to their rooms and I sat in reception with a glass of lemonade. All my jobs were done. Peter Beardsley walked by and asked if I was okay, acknowledging that "Chris can't half hit them." "Tell me about it, Peter," I quipped. "I hope he gets them more on target tonight." This prompted Peter to say: "Oh . . . you know who's in the team, then?" The players themselves were not due to be told until 3.30 pm. "I might," I said. "Then again," I added, trying to keep a straight face, "I might not." At this, he sat down beside me, but I said: "You should be in your room." He asked: "Do I need to rest, then?" "You are bloody quick, Beardo," I replied.

Part of my job involved getting all the team kit ready, at the back of the truck ready for transferring to the team coach ahead of a game. So, yes, I did know in advance - had to - who was in the team. But I was supposed to be sworn to secrecy. Peter persisted: "Oh come on, I won't say a word." I got him to agree that this conversation "hadn't taken place," that we hadn't exchanged a single word today – and then said: "I'm going to the toilet in a minute. The key to the truck is there – in the vehicle – and there's a neat pile of team shirts just inside, at the back. If your squad number happens to be on one of these shirts, then you can work it out for yourself. Then leave the key inside the door and get to your room!" He stood up, gave me a knowing look and shook my hand.

So far as I was concerned, the game could not come quickly enough now. I checked once more with Adrian and then went looking for Glen Kirton, the senior FA official who had our tickets for the big match. Even the well-known England gofer (that's me) had to have a ticket for it. I eventually found him and he handed me the precious piece of printed paper. So everything was sorted now and we just had to run the clock down. It was a glorious afternoon, so I took myself back into Asti once more – for what would be the last such trip. It seemed there were smiles and waves for me everywhere – people could tell I was English and of course there was heightened awareness of our big match upcoming.

One more light meal at the hotel – complete, of course, with yet more tagretelli – followed. The team had to be at the Stadio-delle-Alpi (Stadium of the Alps), home of Juventus, in Turin, before 6 pm. By that time, according to the strict FIFA rules, both teams had to name their line-ups. So everyone had to be on the coach by 5 pm. I stood at the front of it as the players trooped on. This was another proud moment for me, as they all shook my hand on the way to their seats. Most of them added: "We'll get you to Rome." They all knew how much I had dreamed of seeing England in the final. To be doing this – shaking the players' hands and sharing their coach, just two-and-a-half hours away from their participation in a World Cup semi-final – all seemed a bit surreal somehow. It was not quite the same as watching it on the TV set back home!

The last person to climb aboard was Bobby. He looked at me and asked: "You okay, James?" As he did so, he put one hand on my shoulder, smiled and shook my hand. What a giant of a man. I must admit – at that point, I had a lump in my throat the size of a cricket ball. Everyone and everything we needed – thanks in no small measure to myself – was now on this coach. We were on our way. It was a 30-mile drive and once again it was a mini-nightmare. The police outriders seemed to confuse everyone, including our own driver. I knew how he must have felt because I had personally encountered these outriders – you were better off without them!

Traffic was heavy, but we still made it to the stadium in good time. The coach manoeuvred into the complex, beneath the actual main structure. I was last off and I now faced what I knew would be the tricky bit for me. Bizarrely, I had somehow to find my way out of the stadium again and present myself at the turnstile with my ticket, so that I could have "proper" access to the stadium and find my way to my seat. I could not go in through the players' and officials' doors as mere gofers only had match tickets, as distinct from FIFA passes! I talked my way out, past the police.

Now to find those turnstiles. I was just walking around outside the stadium, looking in awe at the vast structure, when I saw a famous face walking towards me. It was none other than Jonathan King. That's right, the singer-songwriter, record producer, music entrepreneur and TV and radio presenter! I had just been thinking how relatively quiet everywhere seemed, with not as many crowds as I would have expected, just 90 minutes from kick-off, but these thoughts were temporarily parked to one side as Mr King, wearing a tee shirt, baseball cap, red jeans and a big smile, swung into view. I was wearing a blazer and the official FA tie – which I assume is what made him stop and talk to me.

We chatted for a good five minutes and I even had a photo taken of me and him together. It turned out he was a very passionate supporter of the England team. Then we shook hands and went our separate ways once more. And so it was back to looking for the turnstiles – and being impressed once more by that wonderful stadium. What really struck me, too, was the amount of public space there was around it – just how accessible the whole thing seemed. The structure itself was awesome. Back in Britain then, we just didn't have anything that came near it – long before the explosion of all-seater new stadiums here. All the Italian stadiums I saw were just brilliant. Ours were so dated and unsafe – make that appalling - by comparison. Even Wembley – the old one, but still hailed as the jewel in our crown – was poor back then. These days, we have so many first class, modern stadiums, with superb corporate hospitality to match – I would like to return to Italy for a fresh comparison.

I made for my seat inside that stadium – and rapidly concluded that if the outside of the stadium had struck me as magnificent, then the inside was just something else again. My seat was located high up, "among the gods," to the left of the half-way line, behind the German dugout. I was all but overwhelmed by the sight of all that lay before me – this vast stadium, which would very soon be hosting such a mega match – and yet I still found time to recall that my Leeds United had played here in 1971, on their way to triumph over Juventus in the two-legged final of the Fairs Cup. Very committed Leeds fan, you see!

I had a great seat, and I kept looking across to the scoreboard on my right . . . and wondering what scoreline I would eventually see on that at the end of the match. The clock said 7 pm now – and still the stadium was nowhere near full. Strange. It was a very nervy final 30 minutes before the kick-off. The dancing girls did their thing pitch-side, but somehow they didn't ease much of the tension!

I had a final bet with myself – England to win 2-1. At last, out came the teams, with the England players – I could tell, even from this distance – still looking very confident, every bit as much as they had done on the coach. The official attendance was 62,628 – some 5,500 short of capacity – and they were to sweat not just because of the lingering heat but also because of an epic clash that turned out to be a much closer, more dramatic encounter than probably any of them had imagined . . .

CHAPTER 21

THE PENALTY SHOOT-OUT –
ENGLAND'S NIGHTMARE

What seemed like a never-ending round of official introductions and ceremonies did finally reach its conclusion and at last – at long, long last – the game was under way. England were playing from right to left, which meant I was closer to the goal they were attacking. How I wanted that net to bulge, with the ball in the back of it, sooner rather than later! Instead, the match quickly turned out to be a very hard, nerve-wracking and close affair, with both teams – these two great rivals - fully aware they were in a battle. It was definitely not a night for the faint-hearted.

Half-time came with no goals. Taking the positive view, we were now just 45 minutes away from the final in Rome! I stayed in my seat for the interval – didn't even go for a drink or to the toilet. That half-time seemed a very long 15 minutes; I couldn't wait for the action to resume. Then the game ebbed and flowed once more, with no-one giving an inch.

Various experts, no doubt, began to speculate that it would take a moment of brilliance – or maybe a freak or a fluke – for the deadlock to be broken. Unfortunately for England, it was the latter – a freak/fluke – that did it. Defender Stuart Pearce – for whom, sadly, this match turned out to be not his finest hour – brought down Haessler 24 yards out. The free-kick was touched on to Brehme. As he shaped to shoot, Paul Parker raced out of the defensive wall – quite rightly – to block. He succeeded with that part of his mission. Unfortunately, though, the deflected shot soared skywards. For a split second, I thought "Well done, Paul." But then I looked on in utter despair as that ball came down . . . over a stranded Peter Shilton just off the goal-line, and into the net off the underside of the bar. What a hideous deflection it turned out to be; what a fluke!

"Oh no, it can't be," I thought. I felt sick . . . but little did I know that I would feel sicker still before this match was over. For the moment, the fans all around me and above were roaring England on. England definitely enjoyed the greater support – not least thanks to large numbers of Brazilians who were still in town after their own defeat in Turin. But I soon noticed that time was fast starting to run out – as it always does when you're losing just by the odd goal.

With just 12 minutes left, England were pushing hard. Platt had a good chance, and then it happened. Parker, appropriately, was able to make up for the earlier setback by sending over a high cross that found Gary Lineker near the penalty spot. He was able to fend off the attentions of two defenders and fire a low shot across the face of the goal and into the right hand corner of the net for the equaliser. All hell broke loose – with jubilation in the English camp! The noise was simply deafening – definitely more so than when the Germans had opened the scoring. The English, the Brazilians and the Italians in the crowd were dancing up and down and hugging each other. I had got chatting to an England supporter who was sat next to me – and, yes, the pair of us, two total strangers, duly sprang to our feet and hugged each other. It was an amazing moment – a moment I will never forget. As if I could.

"We can do this – we can win this now," I shouted, above the din, to the man alongside me. No-one was sitting down any more – even though it was an all-seater stadium! To add to the drama, Gazza got booked shortly before the end of the 90 minutes, which meant he would miss the final if England reached it. Cue those famous tears that the TV cameras picked up. Well, full-time was soon upon us, with the score still at 1-1. So it was into 30 more minutes of nail-biting extra time. It was still hot, but you would not have thought so, the way the two teams continued to slug it out. Then we all thought we had won it when a Platt screamer flew goalwards – only to rebound back into play off the post.

That was the nearest we came, with neither side making the all-important breakthrough. So now it all hinged on those dreaded penalties – with nerves stretching to breaking point. It has always been my belief that the "golden

154

goal" – with the game immediately over once that first goal is scored in extra time - would be a better option, rather than carrying on to the penalty shoot-out. And, sadly for England, I wasn't about to change my mind on that one. Penalties really are a lottery – especially in England's case!

Up first for England stepped the ever-reliable Stuart Pearce – except that this time round he wasn't quite so reliable, seeing his shot saved by the goalkeeper. OH NO! I looked at the ref, clutching at straws and willing him to order the kick to be re-taken (for no good reason!), but no such luck. The night really did not go our way at all. The shoot-out scoreline came to 4-3 in favour of the Germans. Now it was Chris Waddle's turn for England. If he failed to score, Germany would be in the final. Chris, who earlier that day had missed the goal and hit me instead from 12 yards, BLAZED OVER! And that is what it was – ALL over, for England.

Talk about a bad dream – I just could not believe my eyes. There is nothing quite so suddenly shattering and debilitating as to see your side lose a vital football match in that fashion. The sustained drama had kept us on a tightrope for so long and then – in a split second – it's all gone; the dream is over. And you're left with a nightmare instead. You simply cannot believe what you've just seen; you feel as if your guts have been ripped out. In an instant, you are struck dumb and numb. I turned to my new-found companion, whose name I never did get. We just about managed to summon the energy to shake our hands and say goodbye. I can only imagine how all the English fans back home felt, in front of their TV sets. But if it was anything like what I felt, then they endured a truly dark moment.

The one thing we did not feel was that our lads had let us down in any way. They had done their very best, every one of them, but it had just not been our night. Throughout the tournament, all 22 members of the squad had been thoroughly focussed and committed. I had total respect for each and every one of them; they had done their nation proud, along with all their coaching staff and back-up team.

In any sport, it's always a long and slow trip home when you have lost. I have been to many an away match over the years to support Leeds United and the Redruth rugby team – and in the sporting context I can think of nothing worse than such journeys. No matter what the distance, they always seem to take ten times longer than when you have won. So I knew full well what this next journey was going to be like, travelling back on the coach – the 30-mile trip back to our hotel.

The England fans in Italy had been fantastic; I never heard of any serious trouble involving them. Those same fans had endured horrendous travelling arrangements – always having to move some 700 miles or more from base to base. We were left in little doubt that this had been deliberately designed – to reduce the risk of trouble from a yob element, for which English football, and its overseas following, was still unfortunately renowned at that stage. One thing you could say about those who did endure all this travel and constant upheaval – on top of having flown out from London - they were true football fans. These genuine England supporters, who loved their team and their country – and not forgetting me and the team itself, of course - were being punished for the antics of a few mindless morons who had preceded them. I wonder, did this actually cost us the World Cup? We'll never know the answer, but it's a thought, isn't it? Thank you, yobs; you served your country so well. Actually, you are worthy of no country.

In the meantime – rewinding to our defeat by the Germans – I now had to pull myself together and get out of the stadium in order to get back into it, so to speak. I had to repeat the pre-match sequence in reverse – persuading the police to let me back into the un-public part of the stadium. Fortunately, one of the police officers who had dealt with me at the start recognised me and let me back through.

I found the coach and climbed back on board, taking my seat – the second one in – opposite the driver. I was the first back on board, apart from the driver. He was a lovely guy – how I wish I could remember his name – and he commiserated with me. He had already seen his own country, Italy, knocked out by Argentina the day before. Now we must both have had the same thought, because we said simultaneously: "Bari." This was the location for third v fourth place match, which would be England v Italy.

Gradually, the players trooped wearily back on to the coach. Some spoke as they boarded; others were still too choked. I knew we still had a good hour to wait before setting off, to allow for the usual post-match random drugs tests. Sitting close to me were the players I called "the two Stevens." These were Everton's Trevor Steven and Gary Stevens. Not only did they have the same surname – well, almost – but they were both very studious, preferring to study Italian rather than join in card games, for instance. On the way back to the hotel, they were at it again, deep in concentration with their language books. (I wonder how they're getting on with it now! Did they ever reach fluency?) I looked at them and I thought: "This isn't real. Here we are, having just lost one of the biggest matches in England's history, with the wretched penalty shoot-out, and they're already back into their Italian language books."

I looked around and noted the gloom and despondency which, quite predictably, had engulfed the coach. I knew there would be a lovely meal awaiting us, as always, and I gradually began to think: "I'm going to lift this gloom. After the meal, I'm going to organise a party! These lads deserve it. They've done nothing wrong; on another night, they could have won it. No-one at the start of this World Cup campaign, some two years earlier, would have expected them to have come within a whisker of reaching the final."

I know that Stuart Pearce went straight to his room on arrival back at the hotel. He blamed himself for the defeat – which he had no right to do – and I believe he still does. Taking part was not enough; Stuart is and always has been a winner, and nothing else will do.

During that meal, I went over to Bobby and asked if we could have a small party. He unhesitatingly agreed, adding; "I will leave you in charge – the responsibilities will be yours." This thinly-veiled warning was delivered with a wry smile. So I had been promoted from gofer to head of parties, with responsibilities, haha. I got everyone into the lounge and we were joined by two very welcome "gate-crashers." These were Tommy and Jenny South, who owned a hotel and leisure complex in Essex. Quite a few of the England players had gone there and now Tommy and Jenny had driven over to follow the team in Asti. I learnt that the players had invited them into the hotel to join them – and of course they were most welcome to join them in the party. It must have been a good party – for Tommy and Jenny left me with an open invitation to stay at their hotel for nothing. That's an invitation I have still to take up, but I must do so one day!

The party lasted until 3 am – and amazingly I was wide awake again, and up and about once more, just three-and-a-half hours later – barely half an hour later than usual. Another long day, and journey, lay ahead. The big drama of the "main event" might have been over, but this final trip, and all that followed before our return home, was to prove anything but boring.

CHAPTER 22

WARM WELCOMES,
AND SO MANY HANDSHAKES,
AHEAD OF THE THIRD-PLACE
MATCH IN BARI

Seeing me at breakfast, Bobby Robson seemed genuinely concerned as to whether I was ready for the 800-mile drive to Bari. "Are you sure you're okay?" he asked. "Yes, Bobby, I'm fine," I replied, looking him squarely in the eye. "Okay, I'll see you there, don't get lost . . . what time do you think you'll arrive?" "About 8.30 pm, I should think." It was fully 800 miles away, maybe even a little further. Before leaving, I went to find my "vision of beauty," the petite, dark-haired Chinese Italian barmaid. We said our fond farewells and I gave her a big hug. Tears flowed down her cheeks.

My baggage this time also included a host of gifts that had been presented to the England players by various civic dignitaries along the way. I was also annoyed to learn of an unwelcome extra item of baggage – the human variety. For such a long journey, Bobby had suggested that I should have some company, and so, unusually, I had a passenger, in the form of Paul Clarke, who was a clerk with my employers, European and General Shipping. Initially, I had nothing personal against Paul; it was just that I was always happiest on my own when travelling long distances like this. I didn't like having someone else in the cab with me. Even to this day, I don't. Anyway, as it was going to be such a long – and very hot – trip to Bari, I thought: "Ah well, at least he can maybe give me a couple of hours' break and take over with a bit of the driving." I had, after all, only had three-and-a-half hours' sleep.

After stopping just outside Pescusa for lunch, an ice-cold drink and a shower, I said to Paul, while we were still sat at a table outside the motel: "Right, you can drive for the next two hours; I can do with a break."

To my amazement, he replied: "I can't."

"W-hat?" I asked. "What do you mean, you can't? You're here; you're here to help me – not me to help you."

But he just reiterated: "I can't, mate."

I looked at him in disbelief . . . while he just stared down at his bottle of Coke. Then it all came out: "I've lost my licence, a month or so back; I was over the limit."

I was speechless. Here was a man who had accepted a job of driving, to help me when needed, knowing all along that he had been banned from driving. Right now, I felt like smacking him hard and driving off without him. What a complete pillock, I thought. Without saying a word, I got up, put my own bottle in the bin and walked towards the truck, parked a few yards away. At the cab door, I looked back – to see him still just sat there, with his head bowed. I got in, started up the engine, and looked in the mirror. His stance hadn't changed. I began to pull away – and still he didn't move. I thought how pathetic he looked like that, so I reversed, got out and told him: "I'm only going to say this once. Get in the truck, and we will deal with it." He looked up at me, made to say something, but evidently thought better of it. We pulled away together, and I was still seething.

For the next hour, we sat in silence as we drove along and I pondered on what to do about the situation. Eventually, I spoke. "I've made a decision," I said. I had come to the conclusion that everyone makes mistakes – I had even been known to make the odd one myself, more than once! – and so I said: "Right, Paul, here's what I'm going to do about it." I never took my eyes off the road as I was saying this.

And he interjected: "I'm very sorry, James." "For what?" I replied, "for being found out or for being a complete plonker?" Part of me wanted to smile at that, but I was still too angry for words.

159

"So what are you going to do?" he asked.

"Nothing." At this, I could see him, in the side of my eye, looking on in sheer disbelief – or maybe just relief.

"You're not going to tell Adrian or Bobby," he queried, "or Alan Dee (our boss back home)? Why not?"

"Because no good will come out of it. You might be a complete tosser and, even worse, a Chelsea fan, but I don't want you to lose your job."

"Thanks, James; I'm truly sorry."

"You will be, mate, you will be," I assured him, although I little realised just how soon it would be pay-back time. Just a few hours, as it turned out! The opportunity came as we entered Alberobello, the town that felt more like a village, on the outskirts of Bari, and once more I had the problem of finding the hotel. All I had was its name. Such was the commotion – the noise was deafening - it seemed as if the entire town had come out onto the streets to witness our arrival. They were cheering their heads off and waving their Italian flags wildly. Occasionally, someone would bang the side of the truck – and Paul's face was a picture in all this. He looked absolutely terrified.

My one big priority now was to find a policeman, or police station. I rounded a corner and discovered the latter. I pulled up outside the building and, with the crowds still surrounding our vehicle, said to my passenger: "Right, Paul, take this" – a sheet of paper with details of the hotel – "take it into this police station and find out exactly where we are staying."

"Eh?"

"You heard. Get out and go find exactly where it is that we are staying."

"I can't get out; they'll kill me."

"If you don't get out, I'm going to throw you out – and they'll know you're a coward. The most they're going to do to you is pat you on the back or shake your hand. Haven't you sensed that we are being welcomed?"

So, under duress, he got out. And I was right – the reaction was exactly as I had predicted. He made his way into the police station, and while he was in there I got out and distributed some more of the England football "goodies" that had been with me all the way, precisely for situations such as these. It seemed an age before Paul returned – accompanied by a policeman, who had been despatched to come with us, guiding us directly to the hotel.

There was no let-up in the crowd element on our arrival outside the hotel. There were hundreds of them there, and matters were made worse for me when the policemen on duty at the entrance gates asked me to reverse the truck through. No way, I said, but they insisted, and so I had to edge that truck through the gates, backwards, and making sure I didn't take any casualties among all those excited spectators in the process. I will never forget those scenes.

It was around 9 pm by now – I had been up since 6.30 am, don't forget, and had driven 800-odd miles in the searing heat, after just three-and-a-half hours' sleep. By the time I had got everything sorted, with the much appreciated assistance of hotel staff, another hour had gone by. Paul, meanwhile, had disappeared to his room a broken man, having twice in one day proved himself an utter plonker. I headed for the restaurant, hoping against hope that they had kept a meal for me – which they had. Sure enough, I was greeted by the maître d', who guided me to the table that had been set for Paul and myself – except that there was no Paul. So I dined alone, along with an ample supply of beer.

I was half-way through my meal when up popped David Platt, Chris Woods and Peter Beardsley. "Glad to see you made it, then," they said.

"Yeah," I replied. "It was a long, hot journey."

"Ah well, at least you had some help this time," said Chris, referring to young Mr Clarke. As you can guess, dear reader, it was all I could do to avoid choking on my meat balls when he came out with that!

Then Peter ventured into territory that was to cause me more grief. "I need a favour," he said. "I need a training top out of the truck."

"You'll have to wait until tomorrow, Peter, I'm having my meal."

"Well, can't you just give me the key and I'll get the kit?"

At that, and for the second time in a matter of minutes, I almost choked. They were all looking at me with concern, and I said: "Me give Del Boy Beardsley my keys? You've got to be joking. You'll want souvenirs next."

I saw them looking at each other, and then Peter said: "Go on. Please. We will buy you a beer." (Which actually wasn't much of an offer, as the beer was all free to us anyway.) Anyway, I gave in. I must have been going soft – getting tired of arguing – and warned him: "Don't let Adrian see you."

The three of them had only been gone a minute or two when they returned. "Okay, lads," I said, "got your souvenirs – er, I mean training kit?"

Worryingly, Peter was looking very flustered, and he had good reason to as David, pointing to him, explained: "Peter just broke your key in the lock."

"W-hat?"

Confirmation this time from Chris: "He has."

"Well, go and get it out," I said.

"How?" asked Peter.

"I don't know . . . how did you manage to break it?"

"It just broke off."

"Oh, Peter," I conceded wearily. "Leave it with me. I'll sort it out later. Just let me finish my dinner for now."

"Sorry, James," said Peter. "I will buy you two beers tomorrow."

"Bugger off," I said.

On finishing my meal, I headed straight for my room and a shower and a well-earned night's sleep. I drifted off with thoughts of acquiring a hacksaw in the morning, to tackle the broken key problem, and getting a new lock.

When I awoke the next morning, it was to the accompaniment not of the usual "sound of silence", or waves gently breaking in the distance, but of hundreds of soccer fans congregating once more outside the hotel gates. And then it hit me – I looked at the time and saw to my horror that it was 9 am. As if the broken key were not bad enough, Adrian would really go mad with me now, I thought, for being so late.

I quickly showered and shot downstairs. A group of familiar faces were having coffee in the lounge, and Les said: "Good afternoon, James!"

"Sorry, gentlemen," I replied meekly.

But Adrian quickly put me at my ease: "No worries, James," he said. "We let you lie in on purpose; you'd earned it. You go and have something to eat and we'll get the kit for Adrian."

Oh Lord, I thought, so I lied: "Actually, I'm not hungry; I'll get the kit and then I'll just have some coffee."

"If you're sure . . . ?" said Adrian.

"I am."

I almost ran over to that truck and got hold of the lock. To my surprise, there was just enough of the key sticking out to make me think: "If I can just get hold of a pair of pliers now, I should be able to pull it out." So I contacted the hotel's maintenance man, via the staff at reception, explained the situation and returned to the vehicle with the borrowed pliers. The job was easier than I had feared. The broken bit just slid straight out. Thank goodness for that, and I'd have those buggers – Peter Beardsley etc – later. I got the training kit out and returned the pliers to the maintenance man, who seemed very pleased to have been able to help out. I duly reported back to Adrian that everything had been done. (It was a good job I had a spare set of keys.)

I told him I would not be going to that morning's training session as I needed to make a few phone calls to home. I called Mum and, unsurprisingly, learnt that everyone was still grieving. I don't believe football was mentioned once in that conversation – and why would it have been?

Adrian invited me to join him and his colleagues for a stroll into town that afternoon, which was very nice. Among the town's most striking features were its "trulli" (plural for trullo). The trullo is a traditional Apulian dry stone hut with a conical, grey-slated roof. They were generally built as temporary field shelters and storehouses or as permanent dwellings by small proprietors or agricultural labourers, and their golden age was the 19th Century. I had never seen anything like them before. In appearance, they made me think of igloos.

A couple came out of one of them and tried to strike up a conversation with us, which was rather amusing as they could speak little English and we knew little Italian. I managed to understand that they were inviting me into their home, and so, being curious, I went in with them. I was amazed at how much space there was inside – think Dr Who and the Tardis! They made me a cup of coffee and gave me a marzipan biscuit to go with it. They personified the friendliness of this lovely little town. I rejoined the others, who by now were sat outside a café sipping ice-cold beer. They, too, had been inside a trullo. This had been a gift shop – selling, would you believe, miniature trulli among other things! I duly purchased one for myself.

And so Saturday the 7th, the day of the third place match, finally dawned and my mind was a whirl of thoughts about this being the last time I would be doing such-and-such, the last time I would be preparing the kit for these lads, the last time I would be drinking and dining with them, and so on and so on. Everyone had accumulated a lot of extra stuff during the tournament, of course, and so this had all added to their baggage. It was never easy looking after 52 people in this respect, and now we had their wives and friends arriving, too. It could have been a nightmare – if I had let it. Just keep Suzie Barnes away from me, I thought. (Only kidding, Suzie!) I still have that clear image of Suzie panic-stricken as she feared she had lost her luggage, with John getting an earful.

I was beside my truck, talking to Tony Dorigo, when I saw Gazza's lifelong mate, Jimmy "Five Bellies" Gardner, walking towards us. Actually, he walked right past us and went to climb on the back of the truck. "Oi," I said. "What do you think you're doing?"

"Getting Gazza a shirt," he replied.

"Clear off, don't you dare try to get on my truck. Get lost."

He looked hurt, and walked away. I looked around, to find Tony barely able to stand up, holding on to the side of the truck and with tears of laughter streaming down his face. "That was brilliant, James," he managed to say, before another burst of laughter. It turned out that it had all been a put-up job by Gazza. I really liked Gazza. Everyone is aware of his history, but not everyone knew him as I did. I found him a generous, caring person at heart. He loved children and never turned away from a young fan. I have seen him play tricks with children – entertaining them – over and above just giving them his autograph. I hope he gets himself sorted out. A great footballer – live on, Gazza!

The Gazza of today was still light years away when I watched him and the rest of the squad have their last training session before that third place match. At the end of the session, I looked on as Bobby and Don called all the players into the centre circle of the field. I thought: they must be telling them the team for tonight. The conflab lasted about five minutes – and then Don shouted over to me: "Come on, James, come and join us, please." As I ran over, everyone started clapping! Then I realised – it was ME they were applauding! Wow – unbelievable. This was the second time the England football team had applauded and cheered me. (The first time was back in Vietri sul Mare, in the Bay of Naples.) Boy, was there a big lump in my throat now. What a feeling. I clapped back and thanked everyone. And I couldn't resist saying to Don: "I'm playing tonight, then?!" And Peter Beardsley chipped in with: "Go on, boss, let him!" I then joined in a 20-minute kickabout with the lads. Awesome. I tried getting the ball off Chris Waddle. Impossible. I did manage to dispossess Don, though. Mind you, he was into his 50s by now! Then Don blew the final whistle, to bring the session to an end, and everyone shook my hand. How I miss those lads.

I might also say that I miss John Crane's pasta! I was very aware of the "finality" of it all as I tucked into my last lunch with the squad – and, yes, Doc Crane's pasta. How I wish I could have a plate of that pasta today. John passed away in 2009 after serving Arsenal for more than 30 years as team doctor and being with England for four World Cup campaigns – 1986, 1990, 1998 and 2002. He was a very quiet man whom everyone trusted. I never heard anyone say a bad word about him.

CHAPTER 23

ALL GREAT THINGS MUST
COME TO AN END . . .

Still, the presentations, the ceremonies, the speeches, formal and impromptu, weren't over. I thought that would have been it, after the third-place match was over, but I was wrong. It started with the after-match dinner in the hotel, when the Mayor of Alberobello, one of the guests, presented each of us with a gift bag containing two bottles of Italy's finest olive oil, a box of chocolates, and a large book about the region, written in various languages.

There were various other presentations to the players and to Bobby Robson and Bert Millichip – and then it was my turn! I was stunned. My face must have been beetroot-red as Bobby presented me with a small box. It contained a beautiful watch – only 23 of them were ever made – and of course I still have it to this day. Then Adrian handed me a white envelope, which I found contained £500.

The drinks flowed and laughter took hold. With the meal over, and the outdoor swimming pool close by, I was suddenly aware of a big commotion. I looked around and watched in wonder as the players lifted the besuited Bobby up into the air and into that pool with a mighty splash.

Alas, on his way in, he struck the side of the pool and cracked a rib. He was clearly in considerable pain but, do you know, that marvellous man never moaned. His own players had put him on the "injury list," but he still took it all in good heart. I spotted an opportunity here to gain revenge over Gazza for the trick he had played on me via "Five Bellies" – and so I duly pushed Gazza into the pool, too. Everyone convulsed with laughter.

And then, the next morning, when I got up at 6 am as usual, I was struck with the thought: this really was IT, all good things really had come to an end, as they always must. I had loved everything about my time with the England team, and I had definitely fallen in love with Italy. But now it was "home, here I come" and, truth to tell, I had missed my family. The job was done and I needed to be home. It was Sunday now and it would be the early hours of Wednesday before I actually was home. No quick flight back for me; I had that truck to drive!

As priority, I had to get to Lancaster Gate in London (then the FA headquarters) to unload everything. But first there was the long journey from the south of Italy to Calais, in the north of France, to catch the cross-Channel ferry to Dover. I listened to the World Cup Final on the truck radio as I was driving along – not quite the same as actually being in Rome and seeing England play there! I cleared the Mont Blanc customs in just two hours – which I thought was amazing, as you could be there for absolutely ages. I also remember stopping for a leak en route and looking back at the Alps. That vista was truly something else – and it still makes the hair at the back of my neck stand on end whenever I think of it.

The Calais customs were also a breeze – just an hour – but would you believe it, their counterparts at Dover were a pain in the neck, a nightmare. Welcome back home, Mr World Cup Man, I thought. They just had to search the truck and open the boxes, didn't they. I was fuming. They even managed to find the cigarettes and tobacco I had stashed away for the boys in Runcorn (I don't smoke myself), and on which I now had to pay the duty. They also opened up Jack Wiseman's bag – cutting off his padlock in the process. Blimey, I thought, he's going to be mad with me for that. "There's no need for this," I told them. "Thanks for your co-operation," they replied. I paid the duty – and they then had the cheek to ask for souvenirs! At this, I just smiled, said "thanks for your help," and got back into my cab. Tossers, I muttered to myself, as I drove off.

I reached Greenwich around midnight and headed for Blackheath, where I knew there was an all-night burger van. I got a couple of burgers, with chips, and returned to my company's base in Greenwich. I parked the truck

167

up against the wall there, ate my grub, and then put my head down for the rest of the night, still in my cab. All a bit different from my five-star Italian life, I reflected. I woke up at 6 am – so what's new! – and this time was bursting for a pee. So I rushed over to the office, let myself in and also had a wash and shave. Again, all such a contrast with what I had become accustomed to.

I drove to Lancaster Gate, did my business there – unloading and storing all the gear and private baggage, with Adrian, Les and David, and knowing that I would have to return in due course in order to deliver all these items back to their rightful owners. This, in fact, read like something akin to a Who's Who of big football players and clubs, viz – Peter Shilton, to his thatched-cottage home (by special request) in Woodhouse Eaves; to Glasgow Rangers, for Chris Woods, Terry Butcher, Gary Stevens and Trevor Steven; Chelsea (Dave Beasant and Tony Dorigo), Nottingham Forest (Stuart Pearce, Des Walker, Steve Hodge), Manchester United (Neil Webb), Liverpool (John Barnes, Peter Beardsley, Steve McMahon), Tottenham Hotspur (Gary Lineker, Paul Gascoigne), Queens Park Rangers (Paul Parker), Derby County (Mark Wright), Aston Villa (David Platt) and Wolverhampton Wanderers (Steve Bull). There was also a return delivery to be made to Maine Road for Peter Swales, then chairman of Manchester City.

After leaving my truck at my employers' Charlton depot, I caught the train back to Runcorn – by now, I felt I couldn't drive another mile! I told them I would return to work on July 17, as I needed some time with my family, which they accepted. It was about 7 pm when I arrived at Euston train station – and a scene of total chaos. Something was up with the signalling system and it seemed no-one knew what was going on. So I found a phone box and told Linda I was going to be late home.

I eventually caught a train that pulled into Runcorn at 2 am – except that it wasn't supposed to stop there. And it didn't – well, not quite! It was heading straight to Liverpool, so I had a word with the guard when he came around. I explained my predicament, hoping to draw on the country's red-hot goodwill for the England soccer team right now, and all connected with it, by telling him how I had been involved. He had a quiet word with the driver – who agreed to reduce speed to dead slow as he trundled through the Runcorn station, giving me the chance to jump for it, complete with holdall bag. My luck remained in as I walked over to the taxi rank – and found one still there, even at that unearthly hour.

I slept right through to midday. Once I was up and about again, it was great to see Linda and Clare. I could hardly put Clare down all day. Time duly flew, and on July 17 I was back at work, explaining to my bosses how I could easily fit the return of all the England baggage into my day-to-day driving programme around the country. On July 25 I returned Jack Wiseman's luggage to his office in Shirley – and, as I knew he would be, he was livid at the Customs' treatment of it.

The next day, I had just the one easy trip for my normal work – to Preston – and so I decided I would take Peter Shilton's things back to him at his home in Woodhouse Eaves. The door was answered by his lovely wife Sue, whom I had met a few times in Sardinia. She made me a cup of tea and a cheese salad sandwhich while we waited about half an hour for Peter to return home. When he came in, he held out his hand – and I knew the pain that was about to follow. I should point out here that I'm all for firm handshakes, but Peter's hands are like JCB buckets, for size and strength. So when you shook hands with him, you felt as if yours had been well and truly clamped in a vice. "You should have given me a pain killer with my tea," I told Sue.

They said I would be welcome to return any time. "Make it a Saturday and you can watch Derby," said Peter, but I countered: "Make it a Sunday and we can have a few beers at lunchtime!" "Sounds good," he agreed. We did just that. I returned around a month later and we went down into the village, making for his "local." Actually, there were something like four "locals," and we visited them all. We duly had a few more beers than we should have done, and I ended up accepting Peter's invitation to stay the night.

One by one, I completed my post-Italia duties. I was a little apprehensive when I headed further north and over the border into Scotland, namely towards the famous Ibrox stadium, home of Glasgow Rangers – bearing in mind that I was once more driving that truck with "England football team transport" emblazoned all over it. My fears grew when the security people at Ibrox asked me to park outside the stadium – in a central reservation on a dual carriageway, in fact. However, on my return, I was mighty relieved to find that the vehicle had not been touched. Driving back through Edinburgh, I found myself behind a double-decker bus, with the upper deck full of schoolboys. Seeing me and what my truck represented, they proceeded to lower their trousers and pants and stick their bare backsides against the bus windows for my benefit! Ah well, I could live with that; it was the closest I came to any trouble, and I survived the experience.

My last port of call, England soccer-wise, was Old Trafford, although I never got to see Neil Webb there. That was a shame, as we had become good mates in Italy – and later on I was also to be reminded of that phrase about "the long arm of coincidence." His first League club, after leaving school, had been Reading – where I had spent some time in the postal service, of course. We had even more in common when, at the end of his football career, Neil, too, became a postman – in Reading! I don't know what he's doing these days, but last I heard, he had gone into transport – just as I did! Maybe I had an influence on him! If you are reading this, Neil, I hope all is well with you.

Everything had been returned to everyone before the end of August. On September 1, I took my then father-in-law, Andy Bain, a lifelong Liverpool supporter, to Anfield to see his team play Aston Villa. I spotted John Barnes (out injured) in the crowd and so headed towards him with Andy. Three of his security bods surrounded me in no time, but John recognised me and said it was okay. He gave me a big hug and I said: "This is my father-in-law; he's been dying to see Liverpool play, but he's never made it until today." The pair shook hands, and Andy told me later: "I'm never going to wash that hand again!" John very kindly invited us to join him for drinks in the players' lounge after the match.

At the end of that year, on New Year's Eve, in fact, I returned to Anfield, only to see my beloved Leeds well beaten 3-0. I was gutted and headed back to Runcorn with spirits at rock-bottom. They were hardly lifted when I took a phone call – on New Year's Eve, remember – from Alan Dee, telling me they wanted me to move back to London in the New Year. "I can't," I said. "I've got Linda and Clare and a baby on the way."

"We'll talk about it on Wednesday, in my office," he replied. I attended that meeting as instructed, but I did not budge and by 2 pm that day my employers and I had parted company.

"What are you going to do now?" Linda asked, when I told her.

"Go back to school," I said. "I've thought it through and I'm going to study sports science at Widnes College." I had in fact been thinking for some time that this was the sort of thing I would like to do. I had been talking about it with Fred and Norman, the England physios. This would be a two-year course, starting in September, 1991, and so in the meantime I went into business with a friend, Kevin Harris, cleaning restaurants and bakeries.

I got my BTEC Diploma in sports science – being one of the oldest and one of just seven, out of an original 27 starters, to finish the course – and in the meantime my family was growing. On June 22, 1991, my second daughter, Carrie-Anne, came into the world. She was born at home – she didn't make it to the hospital in time! We nearly lost her that morning, as her umbilical cord tightened round her throat. There were two paramedics and two ambulance men in the bedroom, but it was the midwife, Ursula, who calmly got the cord free. Mercifully, there was no permanent damage. A year later, on June 27, my eldest son, James, was born – in Warrington Hospital. The same hospital was the venue for the birth of my second son, Matthew, on October 7, 1994.

CHAPTER 24

MORE FAMOUS FACES . . .
BUT FAREWELL TO LOVED ONES

England footballers weren't the only famous people I got to know in 1990! In September of that year, I went up to Ayr for a holiday with Linda and Clare, when my father-in-law, Andy Bain (Linda's stepfather), introduced me to none other than Viscount (Lord George) Younger, as one of his oldest friends. Viscount Younger was Defence Secretary from 1986-89 and a key figure in Margaret Thatcher's Conservative government.

We met in the County Hotel – one of his favourite venues for a tipple – and throughout it all, on this and subsequent occasions when we met again in this fashion, we were always accompanied at the table by two SAS men. I learnt later that there were always two more outside the front of the hotel, and another two at the rear – such was the level of security deemed necessary for a former Defence Secretary. The two at our table never spoke unless spoken to. Politics was never mentioned. George, who had just been appointed chairman of the Royal Bank of Scotland, was fascinated to learn about my time with the England World Cup squad. He was very passionate about Ayr – both the place and its football team.

Two years after my introduction to Viscount Younger, I was shaking hands and chatting with yet more famous people, this time back on more familiar football territory. Howard Wilkinson, whom I had got to know as part of the England set-up, invited me for an insider's view of my beloved Elland Road. In the players' lounge, I duly met many of my heroes . . . including one guy who was very noticeably sitting all on his own and frankly looking a bit glum, seemingly ostracised from his colleagues. This was Eric Cantona, who, it subsequently transpired, was close to moving on to Manchester United, where he became an all-time favourite.

I introduced myself to him and he chatted as best he could – he spoke very little English. Tony Dorigo, by now a Leeds player, tried to explain my involvement with the World Cup squad. We played Everton that day, winning 2-0, and I got the match programme signed by all the Leeds players. These included Gary McAllister, Lee Chapman, John Lukic, David Batty and Gary Speed.

In 1995 – on May 31 – a light went out in my life with the death of my dear Mum at Treliske Hospital in Truro. I loved her very much and I know she loved me dearly, too. (Gail, who knew her long before we married, still tells me even now just how fond Mum was of me.) My Dad phoned me in Runcorn with the news. I knew she had been poorly, but had no idea she was close to passing away. Then, just one week later, Linda's birth father, Jim Kelly, died of a massive heart attack.

In this same year, we decided to move to the Shetland Islands! Kevin Harrison and I sold the cleaning business. Linda wanted to move to Scotland, to be near her Mum, now that she was on her own, and when we saw an advertisement for a property for sale in Mossbank, on the main island, the whole thing sounded idyllic – no crime, and a quiet, peaceful place to raise a family. We made the big move in October, with our new home becoming a three-bedroom, end-terraced property originally built Swedish-style for the oil workers.

I had no job to go to – but secured one within a fortnight. I joined a team that was busy renovating the village – creating new walkways, cattle grids and fencing and so on. That was my work for a few months until, in January, 1996, I moved into a fish factory on the isle of Bressay. This involved processing fish into fish meal and oil. The stench and the filth were awful, and on my first morning there I genuinely did not think I would last until lunch time. In the event, I was there for five years. The money was good, at £800 a week.

Then a friend of mine said he would find me a job at the Mossbank oil terminal at Sullom Voe – the largest such terminal in Europe. Here I began as an electrician's mate, moving on to the black trades as a welder's mate and then a fabricator's mate. I was there for two years, being one of the last to be made redundant. I was actually chuffed to bits when that happened, because it had been like working in a prison in there, the security was so stringent. Once you were inside and the gates were shut, the rules and regulations were stifling. No-one enjoyed working there - but, again, it was good money.

In 2003, it was all change again. I began studying to become a driving instructor. I attended an interview at a Learner Driver Centre in Aberdeen and then started the theoretical side of it. (I am still in the middle of Part II today.)

Meanwhile, my family had grown again with the birth of Andrew in Lerwick Hospital on June 25, 1997. Three years later, Bobby Robson (by now Sir Bobby) came back into my life once more with an invitation to visit him at Newcastle United, where he was manager, and to enjoy a tour around the St James Park stadium. I jumped at the chance – of course! – and also took Norman Richardson along with me. He and I had become good friends since meeting on Shetland (he was a scaffolder in the oil industry) and Norman was a big Newcastle fan.

On arrival, we were guided into Bobby's beautiful private room, with its coffee-making facilities, comfortable furniture and TV. Norman's niece at that time was in a relationship with Newcastle player Aaron Hughes. Norman told Bobby about this – and Bobby immediately asked a colleague to fetch Aaron – but not to say why. Aaron's face was a picture when he joined us – it was Saturday afternoon, an hour before the match, and he had feared he was going to be told he had been dropped from the team! We chatted with Bobby for fully 40 minutes – and then he left, just 20 minutes or so before kick-off! After the match, we met the players in their lounge. It was all a big thrill for both of us – but Norman especially was on a high, as he had always wanted to meet Sir Bobby but had never done so until now.

Every year, it seems, has no shortage of highs and lows, and 2003 was no exception. In June of that year, I received a phone call from Gail (who lived next door to him) that my father was very poorly. I shot back to Cornwall – something like a 12-hour ferry trip to the mainland and another 12 hours on the train. I finally reached Gail's door (she had the keys to Dad's home). It was the first time I had seen her for 14 years – and she looked stunning, hardly any different from how I had remembered her. Straightaway, I fell in love with her again. We had always been fond of each other, and Linda was fully aware of this.

Gail told me how my Dad had collapsed with a stroke in Redruth town centre two days earlier, on a hot day. He remained alive until November 23 – but in the interim period I made no fewer than 22 trips between Shetland and Redruth, always being told that the end was near, only for him to recover each time. He never came out of hospital, apart from the final two weeks of his life spent in a Carbis Bay nursing home, where he died. He was buried with my mother at Berwick-on-Tweed. He was a great man in my eyes, and to see him suffer, to slowly die, was not pleasant.

In September of that year, Gail made the trip in the opposite direction, travelling up to Shetland to see me and my family. Would you believe, the only train she had ever been on until then was the branch line from St Erth to St Ives! She stayed with us for two weeks. For her trip up, I told her I would meet her in Aberdeen. But I knew that she would be going through Newcastle and so, unbeknown to her, I headed down south to that city, with the aim of a surprise reunion on the train there.

I arrived there at around 2.30 pm – but Gail's train was not due in until 5.10 pm. I knew Newcastle United were playing Birmingham City at home – so I promptly ran all the way to St James Park! On arrival, I thought: "I'll see if Bobby can get me a ticket." I asked at Reception for his right hand man – Tony Somebody – and he was there within minutes. I explained my situation and background. It was 2.50 pm now and Bobby was pitch-side, but the guy phoned through to him anyway. Next thing I knew – and don't forget how close it was to kick-off – Bobby was there in person, giving me a ticket. I explained to him what I was doing, with the paramount need to be on that train at 5.10 pm and Bobby's last words to me were: "Whatever you do, don't miss that train." I say "last words" because that it is precisely what they were, for me. I never saw or heard him again; Bobby died in 2009.

In 2005 I moved back to Redruth to be with Gail, setting up home together in a newly-converted terraced house in Back Lane West. Linda and our five children stayed behind in Shetland. I had sorted out a house for them to move to in Redruth, but in the event Linda found another partner in the Shetlands and stayed there with him.

Again, I had moved without any job to go to, but within two months I had received – and declined – nine offers of employment. None of them was quite what I wanted. I eventually joined Dave Willis – in June 2005 - at

Taurus Logistics, based at Parc Erissey Industrial Estate on the Redruth-Portreath road, working as a courier for UK Mail, the job I do to this day. Thanks, Dave, for putting up with me these last nine years! (Gail had been working for Spar, in Redruth's East End, for five years when we set up home together and she is still there, although it is now Co-op.)

She and I were married in 2007 at Camborne Registry Office, with our shindig at the Shire Inn in Praze-an-Beeble. My best man was John McNally. We had met in a pub in 2003. A year after my wedding, I was attending his (to Tamsin Thompson), at the same registry office. Then, a few years later, I was best man to another old friend of mine, Andy Sinclair, who married Lisa Scott at Bathgate, near Edinburgh. We had become pals on the Shetland Islands.

Finally – and fittingly – one more footballing anecdote. One of the greatest Leeds names of them all – John Charles MBE – was a little "before my time," but I did have the consolation of acquiring his autograph in a very special book. John, also of Cardiff City and Wales, had the distinction of being the first British player ever to join a foreign club (Juventus). A book written by him had been a treasured tenth birthday present for me, which I have kept to this day.

So when I was on holiday in Yorkshire with my family in 1999, I went to see Peter Lorimer at his pub in Leeds, taking the book with me. I knew John drank there. I left the book with Peter, with the request that he ask John to sign it for me the next time he came in. A year later, I returned to that pub – and duly collected my book signed by the great man! (John died in 2004.)

This was but one more cherished anecdote for me in a life that has been dominated by sport – as a player, spectator and, unforgettably, as that "gofer" for the England World Cup squad! (I even become a media "punter" for the 2010 World Cup campaign, commenting on England's matches for BBC Radio Cornwall!)

So many magical memories . . . so many marvellous people met . . . and, alas, so many of them sadly no longer with us. To those who are no more, I dedicate this book.

And in the meantime, many more miles yet to travel, many more friends yet to meet . . . ?

FOOTBALL'S "ANTHEM"

Many a song is sung at football matches. There is one above all others, though, which is synonymous with cup finals. It is football's "anthem" – *Abide With Me,* with grateful thanks to Henry F Lyte (words) and William H Monk (music).

Abide with me; fast falls the eventide;

The darkness deepens; Lord with me abide.

When other helpers fail and comforts flee,

Help of the helpless, O abide with me.

Swift to its close ebbs out life's little day;

Earth's joys grow dim; its glories pass away;

Change and decay in all around I see;

O Thou who changest not, abide with me.

Not a brief glance I beg, a passing word,

But as Thou dwell'st with Thy disciples, Lord,

Familiar, condescending, patient, free.

Come not to sojourn, but abide with me.

Come not in terrors, as the King of kings,

But kind and good, with healing in Thy wings;

Tears for all woes, a heart for every plea.

Come, Friend of sinners, thus abide with me.

177

Thou on my head in early youth didst smile,
And though rebellious and perverse meanwhile,
Thou hast not left me, oft as I left Thee.
On to the close, O Lord, abide with me.

I need Thy presence every passing hour.
What but Thy grace can foil the tempter's power?
Who, like Thyself, my guide and stay can be?
Through cloud and sunshine, Lord, abide with me.

I fear no foe, with Thee at hand to bless;
Ills have no weight, and tears no bitterness.
Where is death's sting? Where, grave, thy victory?
I triumph still, if Thou abide with me.

Hold Thou Thy cross before my closing eyes;
Shine through the gloom and point me to the skies.
Heaven's morning breaks, and earth's vain shadows flee;
In life, in death, O Lord, abide with me.

EVENTS IN 1958

BOAC Britannia flies London to New York in a record 7 hours 57 minutes

European Economic Community (Common Market) begins operation

Explorer Edmund Hillary reaches South Pole

Manchester United Munich air crash, 20 dead

Sputnik 1 re-enters Earth's atmosphere and burns up

Gary Sobers 365 not out against Pakistan - 614 minutes, 38 fours

Nikita Khrushchev becomes Soviet premier

Colonel Saddam Hussein and Iraqi army overthrow the monarchy

Test debuts against New Zealand for Dexter, Illingworth and Subba Row

USSR launches Sputnik 3 with two dogs aboard

George Harrison joins Quarrymen (Lennon-McCartney-Best-Sutcliffe)

Great Britain performs atmospheric nuclear test at Christmas Island

Wolves are First Division champions, first of two in successive seasons

Bolton beat Manchester United 2-0 in FA Cup Final

JAMES MALONEY BORN

THANKS

"You should write a book about it . . ." The words were those of **my dear wife Gail.** They were first uttered several years ago now, and she was referring to my life story.

Well, the deed is done. An idea – an ambition – has become a reality. The book has been written and printed, and the time – and the opportunity – has come to say a very big Thank-You.

First and foremost, I must express my sincerest gratitude to Gail, from the depths of my heart, for giving me the idea and then making sure I "got on with it" by encouraging and supporting me every step of the way. I know it's a cliché, but it's no less true for all that – **this book would never have been possible without Gail's help.**

I must also say thanks to three other people.

To **Mike and Janet Truscott, of Golden Replay Biographies,** for their superb professional support in the writing of my story and the technical side of the book's design and production.

And to **Helen Mulhern, of Eventy PR and Marketing,** for her infectious enthusiasm and phenomenal expertise in publicising *"Gearing Up For England."*

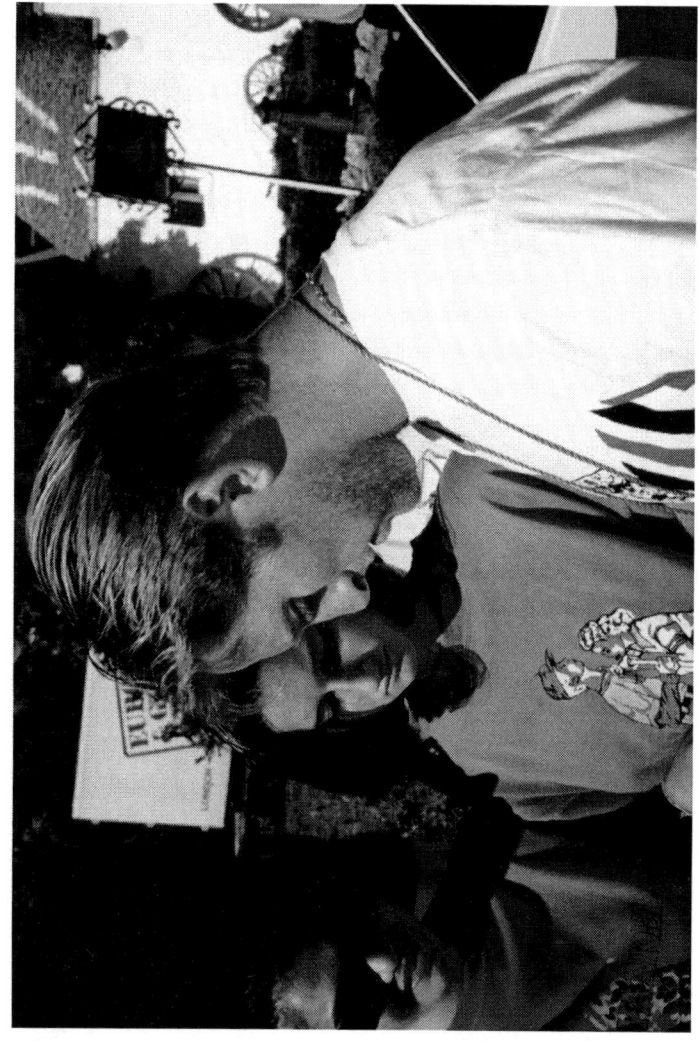

Local autograph hunters in Alberobello.

England make a big splash as not everyone remains dry beside the pool in the party that followed the West Germany match.

Last night celebrations,
left to right: Steve Bull, Paul Gascoigne, David Platt, Gary Lineker, Peter Beardsley.

Me with Andy (Papa) Bane at his wedding to
Linda's Mum, Margaret

On September 26, 1992, I was a guest of Howard Wilkinson at Elland Road when Leeds United beat Everton 2-0. My picture shows Gordon Strachan and David Batty coming off at the end.

With Sir Bobby Robson in his manager's office at Newcastle United. With us are my mate Norman Richardson and his son Connell

Our big day. Just got married to my lovely wife, Elizabeth Gail.

A truly happy moment.

The Maloney future –

Harley and Kayden, my grandsons in Aberdeen, 2013.

Youngest son Andrew with me at Redruth Rugby Club, where you will usually find me when the "Reds" are playing at home.

Andrew with the Calcutta Cup, 2006.

Ticket to glory! My entry into the 1990 World Cup quarter final, when England beat Cameroon 3-2 to reach the semis for the first time abroad.

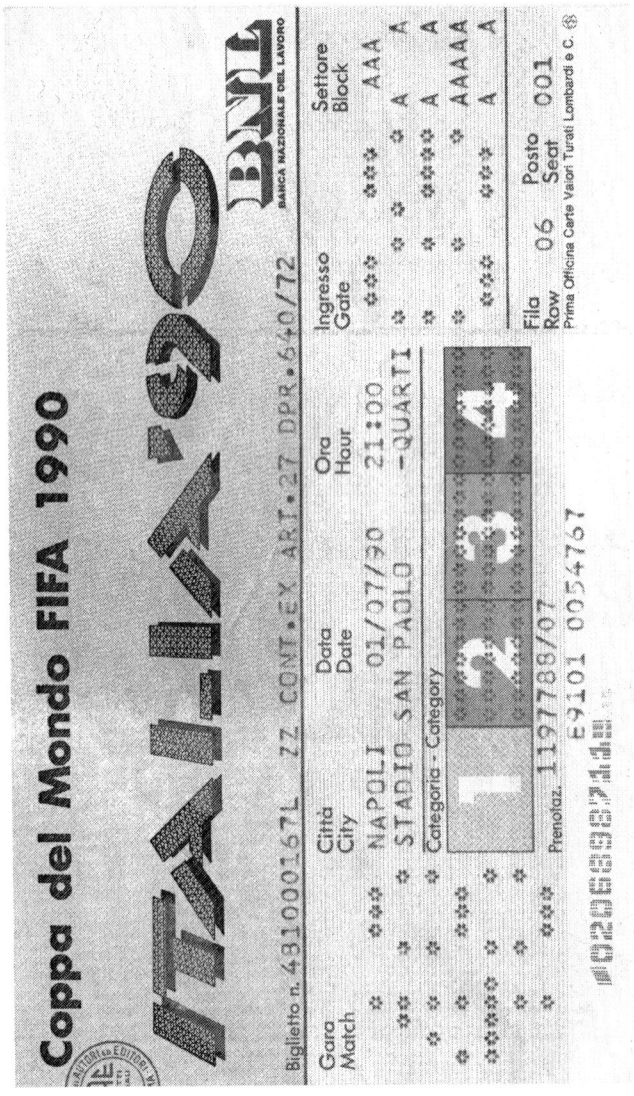

The Krankies were in the pub when I was offered my England job. We already knew each other, so to celebrate they gave me this signed photo of themselves.